AN EASTER SOURCEBOOK:
The Fifty Days

Edited by
Gabe Huck
Gail Ramshaw
Gordon Lathrop

Art by
Barbara Schmich

 Liturgy Training Publications

Acknowledgments

The texts in this book were gathered by Gabe Huck, Gordon Lathrop, Peter Mazar, Gail Ramshaw and James Wilde. We are grateful to the many publishers and authors who have given permission to include their work. Every effort has been made to determine the ownership of all texts and to make proper arrangements for their use. Any oversight that may have occurred, if brought to our attention, will gladly be corrected in future editions.

Acknowledgments for sources not listed below will be found in the endnotes.

Scripture texts used in this work, unless otherwise noted, are taken from the *New American Bible with Revised New Testament*, copyright ©1986 Confraternity of Christian Doctrine, and are used by license of copyright owner. All rights reserved. No part of *The New American Bible with Revised New Testament* may be reproduced in any form without permission in writing from the copyright owner. John 1:5, John 6:33, 2 Corinthians 2:14−16, Revelation 4:3 are taken from *The New American Bible*, copyright ©1970 Confraternity of Christian Doctrine, and are used by license of copyright owner. All rights reserved. No part of the *The New American Bible* may be reproduced in any form without permission in writing from the copyright owner.

Genesis 1:1 — 2:3, Isaiah 12:2, Jeremiah 31:8−13, Acts 1:6−11 and Ephesians 1:15−23 are taken from the *Revised Standard Version Bible*, copyright ©1946, 1952, 1971 by the Division of Christian Education of the National Council of the Churches of Christ in the U.S.A. as emended in the *Lectionary for the Christian People*, cycles A, B and C, copyright 1986, 1987 and 1988, Pueblo Publishing Company, Inc. Used with permission.

Editorial assistant: Theresa Pincich.
Production: Jane Caplan, Phyllis Martinez.
Series design format: Michael Tapia.

Contents

Introduction   vii

The First Week of Easter: Creation   1

Day 1   Light
Day 2   Waters
Day 3   Earth and plants
Day 4   Sun and moon
Day 5   Fish and birds
Day 6   Animals and humankind
Day 7   Rest

The Second Week of Easter: Table   27

Day 8   Table
Day 9   Bread
Day 10   Wine
Day 11   Milk and honey
Day 12   Paschal lamb
Day 13   Foot washing
Day 14   Leviathan

The Third Week of Easter: Ark   55

Day 15   Ark
Day 16   Two by two
Day 17   Flood
Day 18   Dove
Day 19   Olive branch
Day 20   New land
Day 21   Rainbow

The Fourth Week of Easter: Pasture   71

Day 22   Pasture
Day 23   Shepherd
Day 24   Stream
Day 25   Gate

Day 26   Wolf and lamb
Day 27   Ram
Day 28   Apocalyptic lamb

The Fifth Week of Easter: Garden   91

Day 29   Garden
Day 30   Enclosure
Day 31   Tree of life
Day 32   Lovers courting
Day 33   Lovers married
Day 34   Flowers and fruits
Day 35   Well

The Sixth Week of Easter: Palace   111

Day 36   Palace
Day 37   Throne
Day 38   Banquet
Day 39   Heir
Day 40   Crown
Day 41   Shield
Day 42   Fountain

The Seventh Week of Easter: Temple   131

Day 43   Temple
Day 44   Holy things
Day 45   Water
Day 46   Altar
Day 47   Priests
Day 48   Cloud
Day 49   Fire and Wind

Pentecost   151

Day 50   Holy city

An Order for Daily Prayer   159

Endnotes   165

Introduction

HERE ARE TEXTS to help in keeping the fifty days of Eastertime, the great *pentecost*, the space of rejoicing. They are drawn from sources new and old to cast light on the liturgy and the life of these days and to assist in communal and private prayer. It was anciently so: those who had been baptized and anointed and admitted to the table at Easter were led, during the fifty days which followed, more deeply into the mysteries which they had now entered.

Here are some of the words to help this *mystagogia*, this unfolding of the mystery of God and church, take place. They are arranged within the fifty days of Eastertime. Each day begins with a single verse from scripture. This verse is like an invitation to see and marvel at yet one new name Christians have learned and have treasured. After the verse come long and short texts from various places and times. All these texts then, arranged within the weeks of Eastertime, lead us into the meaning of our baptism, lead us to the table. They show us the world under the light of Easter.

HERE ARE TEXTS to lead us into the risen Christ and so into God.

These texts are meant for the neophyte, come this Easter to the waters of life. They are meant for all of us who in this paschal observance are creeping back to those same merciful waters which poured over us. The texts flow from the first day, Easter Sunday, to the fiftieth day, Pentecost. Used singly, these texts may become a source of reflection in creative counterpoint to the church's assemblies for liturgy and for teaching. Used within a pattern for daily prayer, such as the one provided at the close of this book, the texts may themselves contribute to communal liturgy or to the prayers of an individual or household. In this latter case the book becomes a prayerbook for the newly baptized Christian and for us all.

When the order for daily prayer is used (see page 159), one should note that either a simpler pattern marked with ■ (call to prayer, verse of the day, meditation, prayer for the week), or a fuller pattern (call to prayer, psalm, verse of the day, meditation, silence, canticle, intercessions, prayer for the week) may be followed. Into either pattern is then inserted (as "verse of the day") the biblical passage quoted at the outset of the material for each day and (as "meditation") one or more of the longer quotations included for that day.

HERE ARE TEXTS for prayer in the church of the risen Christ.

But how shall we find words for the resurrection? How are we able to bring to expression the conquest of death and the harrowing of hell and the washing which has joined us to God's own life? There are no words. Or, rather, there are only the wrong words—metaphors, chains of images, verbal icons—which invite us into the mystery which is beyond words. So, in the book which follows, the resurrection is the new creation, the great feast, the ark come through the flood, a rich pasture, a lovers' garden, the eternal palace, the heavenly temple, and the city that has awaited our return for years. It follows that to be baptized is to be re-created, to come to the table, to survive the flood, to hear the voice of the shepherd, to be beloved of God, to be heir to the throne and priest to the temple and citizen of the Spirit-formed city. And the risen one is the word of creation and light itself and table and bread and lamb and rainbow and olive branch and shepherd and stream and tree of life and well and heir and shield and temple and priest and center point of the city. In short, as Damasus says at the end of this book, "Jesus Christ is everything."

While this book thus joins the modern quest to find images adequate to speak of God and of whole human life, the antiquity of many of the texts found here demonstrates that we have rich company in our quest. Already the pattern of readings in the liturgy of Eastertime proposes to us that life in Christ is seeing the wounds of Christ at table (in the second week), encountering the good shepherd (in the fourth week), adoring the ascended Lord (in the sixth week), and coming into the city of the Spirit's descent (on the fiftieth day). Such language fills the liturgy! An introduction into the mysteries of the church and into the spirit of the liturgy is also an introduction into such language.

HERE ARE TEXTS which may function as a primer for the sacred speech of prayer.

What is intended in the images of this book is not an exhaustive and reasoned essay on the meaning of the resurrection. What is intended? Windows and doorways opening into the mystery of life given us through our baptism into the passion of Jesus Christ. In each week's cycle of images, there always comes some water image, meant to evoke baptism as our continual introduction into God's mercy. And so, too, throughout these Easter weeks, some note of suffering recurs: the risen one still bears the wounds, and the bringing of risen life into human suffering is the very mercy of God in which we live.

Each week's images are clustered around a central image, proposed first on Sunday. The second week of Eastertime has us, the baptized, brought to the table of salvation; the seventh week leads us to the heavenly temple. Then our imagination explores: We taste the foods and find that even ancient Leviathan is served up for us to eat there. Or we become the priests and walk about the altar under the cloud and the fire. Sometimes these images follow patterns, as in the first week of Easter when the seven days of creation are recapitulated in the risen Christ. Sometimes the images are like chains, as when palace becomes temple which becomes city. Sometimes they are like events, as when "crown" occurs on the fortieth day, Ascension Day.

When one is unfamiliar with such liturgical and symbolical language, some suggestions for its use might not be out of place: Hold together in your mind the image proposed, the biblical verse for the day, and the play of the meditations. Remember that it is Easter. You stand before God in the risen Christ, among Christ's people. You are baptized. Let the words become a doorway into the feast, which is filled with Christ. Listen to the words. It may be the risen one who is spoken about. And it may also be the baptized people, the church, who have been made alive by the resurrection. It may be your own heart. It may be the God before whom we stand.

These all are part of the feast. So, for example—would to God that there were a temple, a place where humanity might be face to face with the true God and where the mercy which promises to wipe away all tears and to speak all justice might at last be known as dwelling in the earth. In the resurrection of Jesus Christ that temple is built. It is present just where we thought it was absent, in the midst of the places of human need and injustice and death. You have been washed into Christ, and so you are part of the temple. You are brought to the holy things. Here is the altar and the fire and the water to heal all things. Here is the very presence of God. Jesus Christ is the temple.

Finally, the greatest image for the resurrection and the baptized life is not a verbal image, but is the very days themselves: Our fifty days of Eastertime, our *pentecost*, is a week of weeks and a final great eighth day, a jubilee, a single day that is fifty days long, a foretaste of the everlasting Day of God. Abbot Patrick Regan writes:

> The Fifty Days taken as a unit comprise but a single holy day or feast, at which God gathers his scattered people to himself. He does so by joining them to Christ in the power of the Spirit. For this reason the feast is no longer a mere institution. It has become a person, the person of Christ. Crucified yet risen, he himself is our Pasch. To be gathered together in holy festivity, therefore, is to be gathered into him whose very person is itself the feast now brought to eschatological perfection.

The fiftieth day, the final day of our *pentecost*, the day we call Pentecost, is the summation of the days. It witnesses to all that the days have contained—the resurrection of Christ and the renewal of the earth and life in God and all the meaning of the images—is poured into our hearts continually by the Spirit alive in the community.

HERE ARE TEXTS for the Fifty Days.

Gordon Lathrop

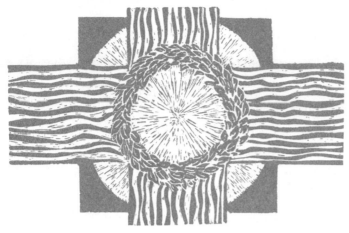

DAY 1

THE light shines on in darkness.

I N the beginning God created the heavens and the earth. The earth was without form and void, and darkness was upon the face of the deep; and the Spirit of God was moving over the face of the waters.

And God said, "Let there be light," and there was light. And God saw that the light was good; and God separated the light from the darkness. God called the light Day, and the darkness God called Night. And there was evening and there was morning, one day.

Genesis 1:1–5

C HRIST is risen from the dead, trampling down death by death, and upon those in the tombs bestowing life.

Troparion
Orthodox liturgy

F LAME, which is a figure for the soul, is also a figure for the living God; for "God is light and in him there is no darkness." As the flame radiates light so God radiates truth, and the soul by receiving truth is united with God, as our eyes by seeing its light are united with the flame. And, as the flame radiates heat, so does God radiate the warmth of goodness; and as the hand and the cheek by perceiving the warmth become one with the flame, so whoever loves God becomes one with him in goodness. But also, just as the candle remains free and disengaged in its place, so does God abide unmoved "dwelling in unapproachable light."

Flame, emitting light, emitting heat, is an image to us of the living God.

All this comes very much home to us on Holy Saturday when the Easter candle, which symbolizes Christ, is lighted. Three times, each time in a higher tone, the deacon sings "Lumen Christi." . . . At once every lamp and candle in the church is lighted from it, and the whole building is alight and aglow Romano Guardini   with the radiance and warmth of God's presence.

O Splendor of the Father's light
That makes our daylight lucid, bright;
O Light of light and sun of day,
Now shine on us your brightest ray.

True Sun, break out on earth and shine
In radiance with your light divine;
By dazzling of your Spirit's might,
Oh, give our jaded senses light.

The Father sends his Son, our Lord,
To be his bright and shining Word;
Ambrose   Come, Lord, ride out your gleaming course
Fourth century   And be our dawn, our light's true source.

W HEN the sabbath was over, Mary Magdalene, Mary, the mother of James, and Salome bought spices so that they might go and anoint him. Very early when the sun had risen, on the first day of the week, they came to the tomb. They were saying to one another, "Who will roll back the stone for us from the entrance to the tomb?" When they looked up, they saw that the stone had been rolled back; it was very large. On entering the tomb they saw a young man sitting on the right side, clothed in a white robe, and they were utterly amazed. He said to them, "Do not be amazed! You seek Jesus of Nazareth, the crucified. He has been raised; he is not here. Behold, the place where they laid him. But go and tell his disciples and Peter, 'He is going before you to Galilee; there you will see him, as he told you.' " Then they went out and fled from the tomb, seized with trembling and bewilderment. They said nothing to anyone, for they were afraid.   Mark 16:1–8

T HE people say that the sun dances on this day in joy for a risen Saviour.

Old Barbara Macphie at Dreimsdale saw this once, but only once, during her long life. And the good woman, of high natural intelligence, described in poetic language and with religious fervour what she saw or believed she saw from the summit of Benmore:

"The glorious gold-bright sun was after rising on the crests of the great hills, and it was changing colour—green, purple, red, blood-red, white, intense-white, and gold-white, like the glory of the God of the elements to the children of men. It was dancing up and down in exultation at the joyous resurrection of the beloved Saviour of victory.

"To be thus privileged, a person must ascend to the top of the highest hill before sunrise, and believe that the God who makes the small blade of grass to grow is the same God who makes the large, massive sun to move."   Alexander Carmichael

O Light Invisible, we praise Thee!
Too bright for mortal vision.
O Greater Light, we praise Thee for the less;
The eastern light our spires touch at morning,
The light that slants upon our western doors at evening,
The twilight over stagnant pools at batflight,
Moon light and star light, owl and moth light,
Glow-worm glowlight on a grassblade.
O Light Invisible, we worship Thee!

We thank Thee for the lights that we have kindled,
The light of altar and of sanctuary;
Small lights of those who meditate at midnight
And lights directed through the coloured panes of
    windows
And light reflected from the polished stone,
The gilded carven wood, the coloured fresco.
Our gaze is submarine, our eyes look upward
And see the light that fractures through unquiet water.
We see the light but see not whence it comes.
O Light Invisible, we glorify Thee!

In our rhythm of earthly life we tire of light. We are glad
    when the day ends, when the play ends; and ecstasy is
    too much pain.
We are children quickly tired: children who are up in the
    night and fall asleep as the rocket is fired; and the day is
    long for work or play.
We tire of distraction or concentration, we sleep and are
    glad to sleep,
Controlled by the rhythm of blood and the day and the
    night and the seasons.
And we must extinguish the candle, put out the light and
    relight it;
Forever must quench, forever relight the flame.

Therefore we thank Thee for our little light, that is dappled
  with shadow.
We thank Thee who has moved us to building, to finding,
  to forming at the ends of our fingers and beams of our
  eyes.
And when we have built an altar to the Invisible Light, we
  may set thereon the little lights for which our bodily
  vision is made.
And we thank Thee that darkness reminds us of light.
O Light Invisible, we give Thee thanks for Thy great glory!   T. S. Eliot

I T is on Sunday that we all assemble, because Sunday is the
  first day: the day on which God transformed darkness and
matter and created the world, and the day on which Jesus
Christ our Savior rose from the dead. He was crucified on the
eve of Saturn's day, and on the day after, that is, on the day of
the sun, he appeared to his apostles and disciples and taught   Justin
them what we have now offered for your examination.   Second century

DAY 2

Y OU fixed the earth upon its foundation; with the ocean,
  as with a garment, you covered it.

A ND God said, "Let there be a firmament in the midst of the waters, and let it separate the waters from the waters." And God made the firmament and separated the waters which were under the firmament from the waters which were above the firmament. And it was so. And God called the firmament Heaven. And there was evening and there was morning, a second day.

Genesis 1:6–8

S O it is right and proper that we celebrate the days of Easter with joy. I will admit to having kept my children out of school on Easter Monday for years. The school holidays before Easter were steeped in preparations and anticipation. Now we needed time for rejoicing. I think the children liked that Monday holiday especially; it was so unlike us to take a "well day" off work and school.

On Easter Monday we have gone to an early Mass to hear the delightful gospel and the Alleluias again. Then we have always found a body of water to visit and enjoy—a river, a lake, a stream, the marshes—fresh, life-giving waters like that which were blessed at the Easter Vigil, like the waters of our baptism which we remember at this time. The story of Emmaus seems to inspire a walk in nature. We see the evidence of transformation all around us in the new green of springtime.

When the children were small we would plan to meet another family or two, usually by the marsh waters near our home. That was the favorite Easter Monday picnic place. The marsh birds were actively expressing their rites of spring and with bird books and field glasses we would identify them and watch them nest. Sometimes there were baby ducks to feed.

Always we got wet. We learned about the traditions of getting wet on Easter Monday first from a favorite children's book which we have read and reread for years especially at

Eastertime. *The Good Master* by Kate Seredy tells of an Hungarian family, and the accounts of their Easter celebrations especially caught our interest. On Easter Monday, the young boys of the Hungarian villages went from house to house, and wherever young girls lived, they came up to the door, recited a blessing and then splashed the girls with water. The girls in turn invited them in and everyone feasted on Easter specialities, and the girls gave the boys some of their carefully painted eggs to take home. On Easter Tuesday they replayed the whole game in reverse.

Then a Polish friend of mine surprised me one Easter Monday morning with such a wet blessing, and "it took." Our children felt so inspired that it has become a part of our Easter Monday rites at the water's edge.

Gertrud Mueller Nelson

T HEN the LORD addressed Job out of the storm and said:
Where were you when I founded the earth?
Tell me, if you have understanding.
Who determined its size; do you know?
Who stretched out the measuring line for it?
Into what were its pedestals sunk,
and who laid the cornerstone,
While the morning stars sang in chorus
and all the [children] of God shouted for joy?
And who shut within doors the sea,
when it burst forth from the womb;
When I made the clouds its garment
and thick darkness its swaddling bands?
When I set limits for it
and fastened the bar of its door,
And said: Thus far shall you come but no farther,
and here shall your proud waves be stilled!

Job 38:1, 4–11

W HEN Israel came forth from Egypt,
    the house of Jacob from a people of alien tongue,
Judah became his sanctuary,
    Israel his domain.

The sea beheld and fled;
    Jordan turned back.
The mountains skipped like rams,
    the hills like the lambs of the flock.

Why is it, O sea, that you flee?
    O Jordan, that you turn back?
You mountains, that you skip like rams?
    You hills, like the lambs of the flock?

Before the face of the Lord, tremble, O earth,
    before the face of the God of Jacob,
Who turned the rock into pools of water,
Psalm 114   the flint into flowing springs.

DAY 3

T HEN shall all the trees of the forest exult before the LORD.

A ND God said, "Let the waters under the heavens be
  gathered together into one place, and let the dry land
appear." And it was so. God called the dry land Earth, and
the waters that were gathered together God called Seas. And
God saw that it was good. And God said, "Let the earth put
forth vegetation, plants yielding seed, and fruit trees bearing
fruit in which is their seed, each according to its kind, upon
the earth." And it was so. The earth brought forth vegetation,
plants yielding seed according to their own kinds, and trees

bearing fruit in which is their seed, each according to its kind. And God saw that it was good. And there was evening and there was morning, a third day.

Genesis 1:9–13

O God,
you have formed heaven and earth;
you have given me all the goods
        that the earth bears!
Here is your part, my God.
Take it!

Pygmy prayer, Zaire

WHAT a glorious spectacle we witness each year as nature awakens from her winter slumbers! What transformation in field and forest as the pall of ice and snow is blown aside by spring's warm winds and buds appear on tree and bush. If our gaze could but penetrate nature's workshops and see the tremendous activity in every sector, how tiny roots are bursting with life-giving sap, ready at a moment's notice to break forth and form the thick, soft carpet of leaves and flowers upon which spring will make her triumphal entry into the land. Today, as I am writing this, the entire landscape is bleak, gray, dead. But in two months the meadows will be green, the trees will be full of blossoms, the birds will be singing, a sense of joy and happiness and well-being will fill the land. For nature will have come to life again.

It should be one of our objectives to regain this sense of close association with nature. The natural rhythm of the seasons should be a source of constant delight. Every tiny flower, every little animal, the rays of the sun, the chirp of birds, everything that spring brings back to us should inspire sentiments of joy and gratitude over our good fortune.

However, we must not remain on the plane of nature; for us nature is a holy symbol. It is a picture-book given by God to his children in which they may see his beauty and his love; a picture-book which tells of another world which now at Easter is likewise celebrating resurrection, the world of supernatural life within us.

Spring with its transformation of hill and meadow is, accordingly, a great symbol of an event in sacred history and of an event now taking place within the church. Springtime is nature executing her Easter liturgy. Neither poetry nor art can even approximate her grand display. In every corner of her vast cathedral a thousand voices are shouting Alleluia, the voices of creatures that have come to life. Yes, nature holy, sinless, eternal, is holding her Easter rites. Oh, that we had eyes to see this mystery!

Pius Parsch

A tree gives glory to God by being a tree. For in being what God means it to be it is obeying him. It "consents," so to speak, to his creative love. It is expressing an idea which is in God and which is not distinct from the essence of God, and therefore a tree imitates God by being a tree.

The more a tree is like itself, the more it is like him. If it tried to be like something else which it was never intended to be, it would be less like God and therefore it would give him less glory.

For me to be a saint means to be myself. Therefore the problem of sanctity and salvation is in fact the problem of finding out who I am and of discovering my true self. Trees and animals have no problem. God makes them what they are without consulting them, and they are perfectly satisfied.

With us it is different. God leaves us free to be whatever we like. We can be ourselves or not, as we please.

Thomas Merton

A FTER the sabbath, as the first day of the week was dawning, Mary Magdalene and the other Mary came to see the tomb. And behold, there was a great earthquake; for an angel of the Lord descended from heaven, approached, rolled back the stone, and sat upon it. His appearance was like lightning and his clothing was white as snow. The guards were shaken with fear of him and became like dead men. Then the angel said to the women in reply, "Do not be afraid! I know that you are seeking Jesus the crucified. He is not here, for he has been raised just as he said. Come and see the place where he lay. Then go quickly and tell his disciples, 'He has been raised from the dead, and he is going before you to Galilee; there you will see him.' Behold, I have told you." Then they went away quickly from the tomb, fearful yet overjoyed, and ran to announce this to his disciples.   Matthew 28:1–9

I T is impossible to understand what Jesus' rising from the dead is about if we think of it as the resuscitation of a dead man. He is not described as starting life over again. He did not mythically represent new vegetation after the rains of winter are over, or human life perpetually coming forth from the dark womb of earth. He was, for the Jews who first believed in him, the "first-fruits" of a harvest of all the dead. If you had the faith of the Pharisees, his appearance would have startled you, but it would not have surprised you. You would have been stunned chiefly that he was *alone*. That he was risen in the body was something that ultimately you could cope with.

It seems strange, at this distance of years, to try to re-create a world we have such sparse information about. We cannot reconstruct ancient Jewish religious thought and make it ours. We can save ourselves a lot of headaches, though, if we realize how much preparedness there was in those times for the notion of being raised from the dead. . . . After an initial shock no less than ours, pharisaic Jews like Peter and James would think, "God's reign has begun! But where are the others?"   Gerard Sloyan

O that I had a thousand voices
To praise my God with thousand tongues!
My heart, which in the Lord rejoices,
Would then proclaim in grateful songs
To all, wherever I might be,
What great things God has done for me!

You forest leaves so green and tender
That dance for joy in summer air,
You meadow grasses, bright and slender,
You flow'rs so fragrant and so fair,
You live to show God's praise alone.
Join me to make his glory known!

All creatures that have breath and motion,
That throng the earth, the sea, the sky,
Come, share with me my heart's devotion,
Help me to sing God's praises high!
My utmost pow'rs can never quite

Johann Mentzer   Declare the wonders of his might!

DAY 4

Y OURS is the day, and yours the night; you fashioned the moon and the sun.

A ND God said: "Let there be lights in the firmament of the heavens to separate the day from the night; and let them be for signs and for seasons and for days and years, and let them be lights in the firmament of the heavens to give light upon the earth." And it was so. And God made the two great lights, the greater light to rule the day, and the lesser light to rule the night; God made the stars also. And God set them in the firmament of the heavens to give light upon the earth, to rule over the day and night, and to separate the light from the darkness. And God saw that it was good. And there was evening and there was morning, a fourth day.   Genesis 1:14–19

S UNRISE is an event that calls forth solemn music in the very depth of human nature, as if one's whole being had to attune itself to the cosmos and praise God for the new day, praise God in the name of all the creatures that ever were or ever will be. I look at the rising sun and feel that now upon me falls the responsibility of seeing what all my ancestors have seen, in the Stone Age and even before it, praising God before me. . . . When the sun rises each one of us is summoned by the living and the dead to praise God.   Thomas Merton

T HE spacious firmament on high, with all the blue ethereal sky,
and spangled heavens, a shining frame, their great
    Original proclaim.

The unwearied sun from day to day does his Creator's
    power display;
and publishes to every land the work of an almighty hand.

Soon as the evening shades prevail, the moon takes up the
    wondrous tale,
and nightly to the listening earth repeats the story of her
    birth:

Whilst all the stars that round her burn, and all the planets
    in their turn,

confirm the tidings, as they roll, and spread the truth from
  pole to pole.

What though in solemn silence all move round the dark
  terrestrial ball?
What though no real voice nor sound amid their radiant
  orbs be found?

In reason's ear they all rejoice, and utter forth a glorious
  voice;
for ever singing as they shine, "The hand that made us is
  divine."

Joseph Addison
Eighteenth century

THE heavens declare the glory of God,
  and the firmament proclaims [God's] handiwork.
Day pours out the word to day,
  and night to night imparts knowledge;
Not a word nor a discourse
  whose voice is not heard;
Through all the earth their voice resounds,
  and to the ends of the world, their message.
[God] has pitched a tent there for the sun,
  which comes forth like the groom from his bridal
    chamber
  and, like a giant, joyfully runs its course.
At one end of the heavens it comes forth,
  and its course is to their other end;

Psalm 19:1–7   nothing escapes its heat.

A s he passed by he saw a man blind from birth. His disciples asked him, "Rabbi, who sinned, this man or his parents, that he was born blind?" Jesus answered, "Neither he nor his parents sinned; it is so that the works of God might be made visible through him. We have to do the works of the one who sent me while it is day. Night is coming when no one can work. While I am in the world, I am the light of the world." When he had said this, he spat on the ground and made clay with the saliva, and smeared the clay on his eyes, and said to him, "Go wash in the Pool of Siloam" (which means Sent). So he went and washed, and came back able to see.

John 9:1–7

M ost High Almighty Good Lord,
Yours are the praises, the glory, the honor, and
    all blessings!
To you alone, Most High, do they belong,
And no one is worthy to mention you.

Be praised, my Lord, with all your creatures,
Especially Sir Brother Sun,
By whom you give us the light of day!
And he is beautiful and radiant with great splendor.
Of you, Most High, he is a symbol!

Be praised, my Lord, for Sister Moon and the Stars!
In the sky you formed them bright and lovely and fair.

Be praised, my Lord, for those who forgive for love of you
And endure infirmities and tribulations.
Blessed are those who shall endure them in peace,
For by you, Most High, they will be crowned!

Francis of Assisi
Thirteenth century

C HRIST, whose glory fills the skies,
  Christ, the true and only light,
Sun of righteousness, arise,
Triumph o'er the shades of night;
Dayspring from on high, be near;
Daystar, in my heart appear.

Dark and cheerless is the morn
Unaccompanied by thee;
Joyless is the day's return,
Till thy mercy's beams I see,
Till they inward light impart,
Glad my eyes, and warm my heart.

Visit then this soul of mine,
Pierce the gloom of sin and grief;
Fill me, radiancy divine,
Scatter all my unbelief;
More and more thyself display,
Shining to the perfect day.

Charles Wesley
Eighteenth century

O N this day, when the LORD delivered up the
  Amorites to the Israelites,
Joshua prayed to the LORD,
    and said in the presence of Israel:
Stand still, O sun, at Gibeon,
    O moon, in the valley of Aijalon!
And the sun stood still,
    and the moon stayed,
    while the nation took vengeance on its foes.

Is this not recorded in the Book of Jashar? The sun halted in
the middle of the sky; not for a whole day did it resume its

swift course. Never before or since was there a day like this,
when the LORD obeyed the voice of a man; for the LORD
fought for Israel.   Joshua 10:12–14

N o longer shall the sun
　 be your light by day,
Nor the brightness of the moon
　 shine upon you at night;
The LORD shall be your light forever,
　 your God shall be your glory.   Isaiah 60:19

I T is an unusual word that is not native to the English or
　 even the Latin liturgical vocabulary: the word "Alleluia."
As a matter of fact, it sounds less like a meaningful word than
the babbling of a child, and when it is sung with many notes
for the final vowel, this impression becomes even stronger.

"Alleluia" does, of course, have a meaning. It is a Hebrew
word, and down the centuries the church has brought it with
her, untranslated (like "Amen"), as a product of the Jewish
soil from which she herself sprang and as a reminder of her
earliest days. The word is a cry of jubilation meaning "Praise
the Lord," and occurs frequently in the psalms. . . .

But the translation does not explain why the church chose
and retained this word from the Hebrew language of prayer
in order to express her Easter jubilation, even though in later
centuries her own children did not understand the meaning.
I think the church meant to say: "In the presence of the
mystery that we celebrate on Easter, the mystery of our
redemption, our usual intelligible vocabulary is inadequate;

when faced with the superabundant mercy of God we can only stammer in amazement like children."

That is how it is with us Christians: As we gaze at the Sun that has risen high over the darkness and cold of our Good Friday, all well-chosen words are useless. We can only stammer out our Alleluia of wonder and jubilation.

Balthasar Fischer

Day 5

PRAISE the LORD from the earth, you sea monsters and all depths, you creeping things and you winged fowl.

AND God said, "Let the waters bring forth swarms of living creatures, and let birds fly above the earth across the firmament of the heavens." So God created the great sea monsters and every living creature that moves, with which the waters swarm, according to their kinds, and every winged bird according to its kind. And God saw that it was good. And God blessed them, saying, "Be fruitful and multiply and fill the waters in the seas, and let birds multiply on the earth." And there was evening and there was morning, a fifth day.

Genesis 1:20–23

AFTER the maggid's death, his disciples came together and talked about the things he had done. When it was Rabbi Schneur Zalman's turn, he asked them: "Do you know why our master went to the pond every day at dawn and stayed there for a little while before coming home again?" They did not know why. Rabbi Zalman continued: "He was learning the song with which the frogs praise God. It takes a very long time to learn that song."

Martin Buber

(SᴵᵀᵀᴵNG in a tree-)
o small you
sitting in a tree-

sitting in a treetop

riding on a greenest

riding on a greener
(o little i)
riding on a leaf

o least who
sing small thing
dance little joy

(shine most prayer)   e. e. cummings

Tʜᴇ world is charged with the grandeur of God.
    It will flame out, like shining from shook foil;
    It gathers to a greatness, like the ooze of oil
Crushed. Why do men then now not reck his rod?
Generations have trod, have trod, have trod;
    And all is seared with trade; bleared, smeared with toil;
    And wears man's smudge and shares man's smell: the
        soil
Is bare now, nor can foot feel, being shod.

And for all this, nature is never spent;
    There lives the dearest freshness deep down things;
And though the last lights off the black West went
    Oh, morning, at the brown brink eastward, springs—
Because the Holy Ghost over the bent
    World broods with warm breast and with ah! bright   Gerard Manley
        wings.   Hopkins
                                                             Nineteenth century

THE whole bright world rejoices now: Hilariter! Hilariter!
The birds do sing on every bough: Alleluia! Alleluia!

Then shout beneath the racing skies: Hilariter! Hilariter!
To him who rose that we might rise: Alleluia! Alleluia!

God, Father, Son and Holy Ghost: Hilariter! Hilariter!
Our God most high, our joy, our boast: Alleluia! Alleluia!

Easter carol
Seventeenth century

DAY 6

IN wisdom you have wrought them all—the earth is full of your creatures.

AND God said, "Let the earth bring forth living creatures according to their kinds: cattle and creeping things and beasts of the earth according to their kinds and the cattle according to their kinds, and everything that creeps upon the ground according to its kind. And God saw that it was good.

Then God said, "Let us make humankind in our image, after our likeness; and let them have dominion over the fish of the sea, and over the birds of the air, and over the cattle, and over all the earth, and over every creeping thing that creeps upon the earth." So God created humankind in the divine image; in the image of God humankind was created; male and female God created them. And God blessed them, and God said to them, "Be fruitful and multiply, and fill the earth and subdue it; and have dominion over the fish of the sea and over the birds of the air and over every living thing that moves upon the earth." And God said, "Behold, I have given you every plant yielding seed which is upon the face of all the earth, and every tree with seed in its fruit; you shall have them for food. And to every beast of the earth, and to every bird of the air, and to everything that creeps on the earth, everything that has the breath of life, I have given every green plant for food." And it was so. And God saw everything that had been made, and behold, it was very good. And there was evening and there was morning, a sixth day.   Genesis 1:24–31

THOU mastering me
God! giver of breath and bread;
World's strand, sway of the sea;
    Lord of living and dead;
Thou hast bound bones and veins in me, fastened me
        flesh,
And after it almost unmade, what with dread,
    Thy doing: and dost thou touch me afresh?   Gerard Manley
Over again I feel thy finger and find thee.   Hopkins
    Nineteenth century

A Hasidic story: A disciple made the following remark in front of Rebbe Menahem-Mendl of Kotzk, "God, who is perfect, took six days to create a world that is not; how is that possible?"

The rebbe scolded him: "Could you have done better?"

"Yes, I think so," stammered the disciple, who no longer knew what he was saying.

"You could have done better?" the Master cried out. "Then what are you waiting for? You don't have a minute to waste, go ahead, start working!"   Elie Wiesel

F OR I will consider my Cat Jeoffry.
For he is the servant of the Living God duly and daily
serving him.
For at the first glance of the glory of God in the East he
worships in his way.
For this is done by wreathing his body seven times round
with elegant quickness.
For then he leaps up to catch the musk, which is the
blessing of God upon his prayer.
For he rolls upon prank to work it in.
For having done duty and received blessing he begins to
consider himself.
For this he performs in ten degrees.
For first he looks upon his fore-paws to see if they are
clean.
For secondly he kicks up behind to clear away there.
For thirdly he works it upon stretch with the fore-paws
extended.
For fourthly he sharpens his paws by wood.
For fifthly he washes himself.
For sixthly he rolls upon wash.
For seventhly he fleas himself, that he may not be
interrupted upon the beat.
For eighthly he rubs himself against a post.
For ninthly he looks up for his instructions.
For tenthly he goes in quest of food.
For having consider'd God and himself he will consider
his neighbor.
For if he meets another cat he will kiss her in kindness.
For when he takes his prey he plays with it to give it a
chance.
For one mouse in seven escapes by his dallying.
For when his day's work is done his business more
properly begins.

For he keeps the Lord's watch in the night against the
    adversary.
For he counteracts the powers of darkness by his electrical
    skin & glaring eyes.
For he counteracts the Devil, who is death, by brisking
    about the life.

          Christopher Smart
          Eighteenth century

T HE Twelfth day after Passover, the 27th of Nisan, was
chosen in 1951 by the Israeli Knesset as *Yom Hashoah*,
Holocaust Memorial Day. Its date of course varies: usually it
will come within five to eleven days after Easter Sunday.
Rabbi Lawrence Hoffman has written:

> We know that worshiping communities impose their sym-
> bolic universe of reality first and foremost on their structur-
> ing of time. Christian time is Epiphany, Good Friday and
> Easter Sunday; Jewish time is Rosh Hashanah, Yom Kippur
> and Passover. More than convenient markers of months,
> these days bespeak symbolic realities for us. What we
> value most and what we fear greatest we encode with
> temporal specialness. What is not so reserved for commu-
> nity memories to ponder is relegated by our worshipers to
> relative insignificance in our scheme of things. So it
> happens that the Jewish calendar now designates one day
> as Yom Hashoah, "Holocaust Day." Is it too much to ask
> that Christian calendars mark it as well?

> Yom Hashoah is already in the official Christian calendar
> in some places. It should be so universally, and not only as
> one of the many days added through the centuries as
> options (usually disregarded), but as a demanding event to
> which Christians are called after Auschwitz. For Jew and
> Christian alike, Yom Hashoah offers the opportunity for
> more than the expression of guilt. It calls for a ritual
> rehearsing of memory, appropriate confession before
> God, affirmation of the "saved remnant," and dedication
> toward those tasks which our Holocaust memory
> demands.

This day falls within our most festive season, the Eastertime.

Even so, this might be the right place. Within the Fifty Days, within the year's Sunday, there would be something broken—a fast day, a mourning day, a day for renunciations of evil. Such a day would not be so much like a lenten day somehow misplaced. It would be far more harsh. In the midst of Easter it would have to raise up for us every question the holocaust itself raises.

The day cannot, however, simply be put on the Christian *Gabe Huck*   calendar. It must be quietly and humbly begun in our lives.

DAY 7

ONLY in God is my soul at rest.

THUS the heavens and the earth were finished, and all the host of them. And on the seventh day God finished the work which had been done, and God rested on the seventh day from all the work which God had done. So God blessed the seventh day and hallowed it, because on it God rested *Genesis 2:1–3*   from all the work which God had done in creation.

TAKE care to keep holy the sabbath day as the LORD, your God, commanded you. Six days you may labor and do all your work: but the seventh day is the sabbath of the LORD, your God. No work may be done then, whether by you, or your son or daughter, or your male or female slave, or your ox or ass or any of your beasts, or the alien who lives with you. Your male and female slave should rest as you do. For remember that you too were once slaves in Egypt, and the LORD, your God, brought you from there with his strong hand and outstretched arm. That is why the LORD, your *Deuteronomy 5:12–15*   God, has commanded you to observe the sabbath day.

THE meaning of the Sabbath is to celebrate time rather than space. Six days a week we live under the tyranny of things of space; on the Sabbath we try to become attuned to *holiness in time.* It is a day on which we are called upon to share in what is eternal in time, to turn from the results of creation to the mystery of creation; from the world of creation to the creation of the world. . . .

The seventh day is like a palace in time with a kingdom for all. It is not a date but an atmosphere. . . .

[A legend says:] "Angels have six wings, one for each day of the week, with which they chant their song; but they remain silent on the Sabbath, for it is the Sabbath which then chants a hymn to God." It is the Sabbath that inspires all the creatures to sing praise to the Lord.

Abraham Heschel

O Lord God, give us peace, for you have given all things to us, the peace of rest, the peace of the sabbath, the peace without an evening. This entire most beautiful order of things that are very good, when their measures have been accomplished, is to pass away. For truly in them a morning has been made, and an evening also.

Then also you shall rest in us, even as now you work in us, and so will that rest of yours be in us, even as these your works are through us. But you, O Lord, are ever at work and ever at rest. You do not see for a time, nor are you moved for a time, nor do you rest for a time. Yet you make both that things be seen in time, and the times themselves, and the rest that comes after time.

Augustine
Fourth century

THE Lord showed a little thing, the size of a hazelnut, which seemed to lie in the palm of my hand; and it was as round as any ball. I looked upon it with the eye of my understanding, and thought, "What may this be?" I was answered in a general way, thus: "It is all that is made." I wondered how long it could last; for it seemed as though it might suddenly fade away to nothing, it was so small. And I was answered in my understanding: "It lasts, and ever shall last; for God loveth it. And even so hath everything being— by the love of God."

In this little thing I saw three properties. The first is that God made it: the second, that God loveth it: the third, that God keepeth it. And what beheld I in this? Truly, the Maker, the Lover and the Keeper. And until I am substantially united to him, I can never have full rest nor true bliss; that is to say, until I am so fastened to him that there is no created thing at all between my God and me. For this is the reason why we are not all in ease of heart and of soul: that we seek here rest in this thing that is so little and where no rest is in, we know not our God that is almighty, all-wise and all-good. For he is very rest.

Julian of Norwich
Fifteenth century

H OLLA, the Incarnate Son
Hath come to earth and fought and won.

Lullay, he lieth in tomb,
And for my soul he findeth room.

Lullay, I rest in him,
Weary spirit and weary limb.

Holla, we rise;
He leadeth me after him through the skies.

Holla, we compass about and hem
The golden gates of Jerusalem.

Holla, we enter in
Because my friend hath not known sin.

Hallelujah, I see Lord God and all is well;
Lullay, I rest in him.

"The Shout"
Adam Fox

SECOND WEEK OF EASTER

T ASTE and see how good the LORD is.

THE table fellowship of Christians implies obligation. It is our daily bread that we eat, not my own. We share our bread. Thus we are firmly bound to one another not only in the Spirit but in our whole physical being. The *one* bread that is given to our fellowship links us together in a firm covenant. Now none dares go hungry as long as another has bread, and anyone who breaks this fellowship of the physical life also breaks the fellowship of the Spirit.

Dietrich Bonhoeffer

ONE of the brethren asked Master Jordan whether it would be more useful for him to devote himself to his prayers or to apply himself to studying the bible. He replied, "Which is better, to spend your whole time drinking, or to spend your whole time eating? Surely it is best for them to take their turn, and so it is too in the other case."

The Lives of the Brethren

B Y this light I shall come to know
that you, eternal Trinity,
are table
and food
and waiter for us.
You, eternal Father,
are the table
that offers us as food
the Lamb, your only-begotten Son.
He is the most exquisite of foods for us,
both in his teaching,
which nourishes us in your will,
and in the sacrament
that we receive in holy communion,
which feeds and strengthens us
while we are pilgrim travelers in this life.
And the Holy Spirit
is indeed a waiter for us,
for he serves us this teaching
by enlightening our mind's eye with it
and inspiring us to follow it.
And he serves us charity for our neighbors
and hunger to have as our food
souls
and the salvation of the whole world
for the Father's honor.

Catherine of Siena
Fourteenth century

O N the evening of that first day of the week, when the
doors were locked, where the disciples were, for fear
of the Jews, Jesus came and stood in their midst and said to
them, "Peace be with you." When he had said this, he
showed them his hands and his side. The disciples rejoiced
when they saw the Lord. Jesus said to them again, "Peace

be with you. As the Father has sent me, so I send you." And when he had said this, he breathed on them and said to them, "Receive the Holy Spirit. Whose sins you forgive are forgiven them, and whose sins you retain are retained."

Thomas, called Didymus, one of the Twelve, was not with them when Jesus came. So the other disciples said to him, "We have seen the Lord." But he said to them, "Unless I see the mark of the nails in his hands and put my finger into the nailmarks and put my hand into his side, I will not believe." Now a week later his disciples were again inside and Thomas was with them. Jesus came, although the doors were locked, and stood in their midst and said, "Peace be with you." Then he said to Thomas, "Put your finger here and see my hands, and bring your hand and put it into my side, and do not be unbelieving, but believe." Thomas answered and said to him, "My Lord and my God!" Jesus said to him, "Have you come to believe because you have seen me? Blessed are those who have not seen and have believed."   John 20:19–29

T HE table is, beyond all others, the *social furnishing*. It is, to begin with, the piece of furniture made for reunions; being accessible from all sides, the table is made to be surrounded. People avoid setting it against a wall, so that no side shall be rendered useless. Instead, it is placed in the center of the available space and thus can be approached at any point on its perimeter. Here, then, in the center of a common room, the members of the family have a kind of permanent, though tacit, rendezvous. During the hours when the members are away at work, the unused table in the quiet room embodies an invitation and waits for its own specific "world." It is here that the family, daily scattered, is daily reunited. . . .

Together with chair or bench, the support given by the table enables people to sit in great comfort. The level surface, the upper limbs resting on it, and the chest and face rising above it, all mark out for each sitter a space for his personal gestures and for countless possible actions. The physical relaxation of the posture gives full freedom for reflection and speaking. The faces turn to one another and the gazes meet. The hands, freed from toil, can lend themselves fully to the effort of self-expression. Each person involves himself with all the others and communicates himself in the process. Thus the table is the place beyond all others for dialogue between members of the family; they sit there to talk "among themselves," to tell of the day just ending and of the morrow, as, with heads close together, they exchange impressions, confidences, and confessions.

Edmond Barbotin

L OVE bade me welcome: yet my soul drew back,
  Guilty of dust and sin.
But quick-ey'd Love, observing me grow slack
    From my first entrance in,
Drew nearer to me, sweetly questioning
    If I lack'd anything.

A guest. I answer'd, worthy to be here:
    Love said, You shall be he.
I the unkind, ungrateful? Ah my dear,
    I cannot look on thee.
Love took my hand, and smiling did reply,
    Who made the eyes but I?

Truth Lord, but I have marr'd them: let my shame
    Go where it doth deserve.
And know you not, says Love, who bore the blame?
    My dear, then I will serve.
You must sit down, says Love, and taste my meat:
    So I did sit and eat.

George Herbert
Seventeenth century

THE LORD appeared to Abraham by the terebinth of Mamre, as he sat in the entrance of his tent, while the day was growing hot. Looking up, he saw three men standing nearby. When he saw them, he ran from the entrance of the tent to greet them; and bowing to the ground, he said: "Sir, if I may ask you this favor, please do not go on past your servant. Let some water be brought, that you may bathe your feet, and then rest yourselves under the tree. Now that you have come this close to your servant, let me bring you a little food, that you may refresh yourselves; and afterward you may go on your way." "Very well," they replied, "do as you have said."

Abraham hastened into the tent and told Sarah, "Quick, three seahs of fine flour! Knead it and make rolls." He ran to the herd, picked out a tender, choice steer, and gave it to a servant, who quickly prepared it. Then he got some curds and milk, as well as the steer that had been prepared, and set these before them; and he waited on them under the tree while they ate.

Genesis 18:1–8

DAY 9

GOD's bread comes down from heaven and gives life to the world.

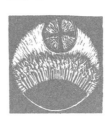

WE had hard baked potatoes for supper, and overspiced cabbage. I'm in favor of becoming a vegetarian only if the vegetables are cooked right. (What a hard job cooking is here! But the human warmth in the dining room covers up a multitude of sins.) Another food grievance: onions chopped up in a fruit salad, plus spices and herbs! A sacrilege—to treat foods in this way. Food should be treated with respect, since our Lord left himself to us in the guise of food. His disciples knew him in the breaking of bread.

Dorothy Day

J UST as the bread is made out of many grains ground and mixed together, and out of the bodies of many grains there comes the body of one bread, in which each grain loses its form and body and takes upon itself the common body of the bread; and just as the drops of wine, in losing their own form, become the body of one common wine and drink—so it is and should be with us, if we use this sacrament properly. Christ with all saints, by his love, takes upon himself our form, fights with us against sin, death and all evil. This enkindles in us such love that we take on his form, rely upon his righteousness, life and blessedness. And through the interchange of his blessings and our misfortunes, we become one loaf, one bread, one body, one drink, and have all things in common.

Martin Luther
Sixteenth century

N OW that very day two of them were going to a village seven miles from Jerusalem called Emmaus, and they were conversing about all the things that had occurred. And it happened that while they were conversing and debating, Jesus himself drew near and walked with them, but their eyes were prevented from recognizing him. He asked them, "What are you discussing as you walk along?" They stopped, looking downcast. One of them, named Cleopas, said to him in reply, "Are you the only visitor to Jerusalem who does not know of the things that have taken place there in these days?" And he replied to them, "What sort of things?" They said to him, "The things that happened to Jesus the Nazarene, who was a prophet mighty in deed and word before God and all the people, how our chief priests and rulers both handed him over to a sentence of death and crucified him. But we were hoping that he would be the one to redeem Israel; and besides all this, it is now the third day since this took place. Some women from our group, however, have astounded us: they were at the tomb early in the morning and did not find his body; they came back and reported that they had indeed seen a vision of angels who announced that he was alive. Then some of those with us went to the tomb and found things just as the women had described, but him they did not see." And he said to them, "Oh, how foolish you are! How slow of heart to believe all that the prophets spoke! Was it not necessary that the Messiah should suffer these things and enter into his glory?" Then beginning with Moses and all the prophets, he interpreted to them what referred to him in all the scriptures. As they approached the village to which they were going, he gave the impression that he was going on farther. But they urged him, "Stay with us, for it is nearly evening and the day is almost over." So he went in to stay with them. And it happened that, while he was with them at table, he took bread, said the blessing, broke it, and gave it to them. With that their eyes were opened and they recognized him, but he vanished from their sight. Then they said to each other, "Were not our hearts burning within us while he spoke to us on the way and opened the scriptures to us?" So they set out at once and returned to Jerusalem where they found gathered together the eleven and those with them who were saying, "The Lord has truly been raised and has appeared to Simon!" Then the two recounted what had taken place on the way and how he was made known to them in the breaking of the bread.   Luke 24:13–35

I N the act of creating a bread, an honest loaf, an object with a presence, a fragrance, a substance, a taste, some would say even a soul, the baker has changed grain and flour and liquid into an entity. She or he has taken yeast, a dormant colony of living plants, and released and nurtured them in embryonic warmth, has sprinkled in sugar on which yeast thrives, has sifted in flour that builds the cellular elastic structure that holds the tiny carbon dioxide bubbles that raise the framework of the house called bread. And in that house is love, and warmth, and nourishment, and comfort, and care, and caring, and taking care, and time gone by, and time well spent, and things natural, and things good, and honest toil, and work without thought of reward, and all of those things once had, now lost in a country and a world that has rushed by itself and passed itself, running, and never noticed the loss.

Yvonne Young Tarr

N OW the green blade rises from the buried grain,
Wheat that in dark earth many days has lain;
Love lives again, that with the dead has been;
Love is come again like wheat arising green.

When our hearts are wintry, grieving, or in pain,
Your touch can call us back to life again,
Fields of our hearts that dead and bare have been;
Love is come again like wheat arising green.

John M. C. Crum

Ignatius of Antioch
Second century

I am God's wheat, ground fine by the lions' teeth to be made purest bread for Christ.

B READ as produced from the earth concentrates within itself all the cosmic forces that were required for its production; through the bread we make, we are rooted in the soil that yielded the wheat and, in turn incorporate that soil into ourselves. Thus bread is not only something to be highly regarded, it is *sacred:* to throw it away, to waste it, is to make light of all the values of which it is the bearer, the human work it has entailed, and the human life it can save.

Edmond Barbotin

THEN let us feast this Easter Day
On Christ, the bread of heaven.
The Word of grace has purged away
The old and evil leaven.
Christ alone our souls will feed;
He is our meat and drink indeed;
Faith lives upon no other!
Alleluia!

Martin Luther
Sixteenth century

DAY 10

I am the true vine.

WE were created to delight, as God does, in the resident goodness of creation. We were not made to sit around mumbling incantations and watching our insides to see what creation will do for us. Wine does indeed have subjective effects, but they are to be received gratefully and lightly. They are not solemnly important psychological adjustments, but graces, super-added gifts. It was St. Thomas Aquinas who gave the most reasonable and relaxed of all the definitions of temperance. Wine, he said, could lawfully be drunk *usque ad hilaritatem,* to the point of cheerfulness. It is a happy example of the connection between sanctity and sanity.

Robert Farrar Capon

T HEY were all astounded and bewildered, and said to one another, "What does this mean?" But others said, scoffing, "They have had too much new wine." Then Peter stood up with the Eleven, raised his voice, and proclaimed to them, "These people are not drunk, as you suppose, for it is only nine o'clock in the morning. No, this is what was spoken through the prophet Joel:

'It will come to pass in the last days,'
    God says,
Acts 2:12–14a, 15–17   'that I will pour out a portion of my spirit upon all flesh.'"

I T was with good reason, then, that some people, when they heard the apostles speaking in every tongue, said: "They are filled with the new wine." For they had become fresh wine-skins, they had been renewed by the grace of holiness, so that when they were filled with the new wine, that is, with the Holy Spirit, they spoke with fervor in every tongue. . . . Celebrate, then, this day as members of the one body of Christ. Your celebration will not be in vain if you *are* what you celebrate, if you hold fast to the church which the Lord filled with his Holy Spirit.

African homily
Sixth century

Y OU soul devoted to God, whoever you are, run with living desire to this Fountain of life and light.

From this Fountain flows the stream of the oil of gladness, which gladdens the city of God, and the powerful fiery torrent, the torrent, I say, of the pleasure of God, from which the guests at the heavenly banquet drink to joyful inebriation and sing without ceasing hymns of jubilation.

Bonaventure
Thirteenth century

SIMILARLY, the wine of Christ's blood, drawn from the many grapes of the vineyard that he had planted, is extracted in the winepress of the cross. When men receive it with believing hearts, like capacious wineskins, it ferments within them by its own power.

Gaudentius
Fourth century

PAUL cried with all exactness of truth, "For if we have been planted together in the likeness of his death, we shall be also in the likeness of his resurrection." Well has he said, "planted together." For since the true vine was planted in this place, we also by partaking in the baptism of death, have been planted together with him.

Cyril of Jerusalem
Fourth century

THE wine of the psalter and the wine of heaven are the same, and they are ours, because whether in heaven or on earth there is only one chalice, and that chalice itself is heaven. It is the cup Jesus gave to his disciples on the night when he said to them: "With desire have I desired to eat this Pasch with you." There is one mystery in the kingdom of heaven, which is the light of that kingdom, replacing the sun, moon and stars. It is the light also of the psalter and of the church on earth, though it shines in darkness. Its light is wine. It was of this wine that Jesus said: "I shall not drink the fruit of this vine again until I drink it with you now in the kingdom of my Father." He had just chanted the psalms of the *Hallel* with his apostles. He knew his blood would flow like silence through our psalter.

Thomas Merton

B UT it is not only the martyrs who share in his passion by their glorious courage; the same is true, by faith, of all who are born again in baptism. That is why we are to celebrate the Lord's paschal sacrifice with the unleavened bread of sincerity and truth. The leaven of our former malice is thrown out, and a new creature is filled and inebriated with the Lord himself. For the effect of our sharing in the body and blood of Christ is to change us into what we receive. As we have died with him, and have been buried and raised to life with him, so we bear him within us, both in body and in spirit, in everything we do.

Leo the Great
Fifth century

O N the third day there was a wedding in Cana in Galilee, and the mother of Jesus was there. Jesus and his disciples were also invited to the wedding. When the wine ran short, the mother of Jesus said to him, "They have no wine." And Jesus said to her, "Woman, how does your concern affect me? My hour has not yet come." His mother said to the servers, "Do whatever he tells you." Now there were six stone water jars there for Jewish ceremonial washings, each holding twenty to thirty gallons. Jesus told them, "Fill the jars with water." So they filled them to the brim. Then he told them, "Draw some out now and take it to the headwaiter." So they took it. And when the headwaiter tasted the water that had become wine, without knowing where it came from (although the servers who had drawn the water knew), the headwaiter called the bridegroom and said to him, "Everyone serves good wine first, and then when people have drunk freely, an inferior one; but you have kept the good wine until now." Jesus did this as the beginning of his signs in Cana in Galilee and so revealed his glory, and his disciples began to believe in him.

John 2:1–11

I eat my honey and my sweetmeats,
I drink my wine and my milk.

L IKE an eagle stirring up its nestlings,
Dashing against its brood,
Spreading its wings to catch them,
And carrying them on its pinions,
The LORD alone was their leader,
And no foreign god was with the LORD.
The LORD made them mount the heights of the earth,
And they ate the products of the field;
The LORD had them suck honey from crags,
And oil from flinty rocks.
Curds from cows and milk from sheep,
With the fat of lambs and rams,
Herds of Bashan and goats,
With the very choicest wheat,
And the blood of the grapes, a foaming draught,
Jacob ate to the fill.

Deuteronomy
32:11–14

T HE deacons then present the oblation to the bishop. He
gives thanks with regard to the bread, which represents
the body of Christ; he gives thanks also with regard to the
cup, in which the wine is mixed that represents the blood
poured out for all those who believe in him. He also gives
thanks with regard to the mingled milk and honey, which
represents the fulfillment of the promise God made to our
ancestors, a promise signified by the land flowing with milk
and honey and fulfilled in the flesh of Christ which he gives
us and by which believers are nourished like little children,
for the sweetness of his word changes the bitterness of our
hearts into gentleness. Finally, he gives thanks with regard to

Hippolytus
Third century

the water for the oblation, to signify purification, so that the interior and spiritual may receive the same effect as the body. Let the bishop explain all this carefully to those who receive it.

1 Peter 2:2–3

L IKE newborn infants, long for pure spiritual milk so that through it you may grow into salvation, for you have tasted that the Lord is good.

Zeno of Verona
Fourth century

W HY do you hesitate? Thanks to your faith, the wave of rebirth has already begotten you. It is bringing you forth through the sacraments. Hasten with all speed to the center of your desire. Lo, a solemn hymn is being chanted. Lo, the sweet wail of the newborn is heard. Lo, the most illustrious brood of the begotten proceeds from the one womb. A new thing, that each one is born spiritually. Run, then, forward to the mother who experiences no pains of labor although she cannot count the number of those to whom she gives birth. Enter, then. Enter! Happily you are going to drink the new milk together.

Clement of Alexandria
Second century

J ESUS Christ,
celestial Milk out-pressed
from a young bride's fragrant breasts
(your Wisdom's graces),
your little children
with their tender mouths
slake their thirst there,
drink their fill
of the Spirit flowing
from those incorporeal nipples.

N OW we're going to march again, and we've got to
march again, in order to put the issue where it is
supposed to be. And force everybody to see that there are
thirteen hundred of God's children here suffering, sometimes going hungry, going through dark and dreary nights
wondering how this thing is going to come out. That's the
issue. And we've got to say to the nation: we know it's
coming out. For when people get caught up with that which
is right and they are willing to sacrifice for it, there is no
stopping point short of victory. . . .

It's alright to talk about "long white robes over yonder," in all
of its symbolism. But ultimately people want some suits and
dresses and shoes to wear down here. It's alright to talk about
"streets flowing with milk and honey," but God has commanded us to be concerned about the slums down here, and
his children who can't eat three square meals a day. It's
alright to talk about the new Jerusalem, but one day, God's
preacher must talk about the New York, the new Atlanta, the
new Philadelphia, the new Los Angeles, the new Memphis,
Tennessee. This is what we have to do.   Martin Luther King, Jr.

O H, that you may suck fully
of the milk of her comfort,
That you may nurse with delight
    at her abundant breasts!   Isaiah 66:11

I saw a brazen ladder of wondrous length reaching up to
heaven, but so narrow that only one could ascend at once;
and on the sides of the ladder were fastened all kinds of iron
weapons. There were swords, lances, hooks, daggers, so
that if any one went up carelessly or without looking
upwards he was mangled and his flesh caught on the
weapons. And just beneath the ladder was a dragon

couching of wondrous size who lay in wait for those going up and sought to frighten them from going up. Now Saturus went up first, who had given himself up for our sakes of his own accord, because our faith had been of his own building, and he had not been present when we were seized. And he reached the top of the ladder, and turned, and said to me: "Perpetua, I await you; but see that the dragon bite you not." And I said: "In the name of Jesus Christ he will not hurt me." And he put out his head gently, as if afraid of me, just at the foot of the ladder; and as though I were treading on the first step, I trod on his head. And I went up, and saw a vast expanse of garden, and in the midst a man sitting with white hair, in the dress of a shepherd, a tall man, milking sheep; and round about were many thousands clad in white. And he raised his head, and looked upon me, and said: "You have well come, my child." And he called me, and gave me a morsel of the milk which he was milking and I received it in my joined hands, and ate; and all they that stood around said: "Amen." And at the sound of the word I woke, still eating something sweet.

Perpetua
Second century

DAY 12

T HERE is the Lamb of God.

W HAT wondrous love is this, O my soul, O my soul?
What wondrous love is this, O my soul?
What wondrous love is this that caused the Lord of bliss
to lay aside his crown for my soul, for my soul,
to lay aside his crown for my soul?

To God and to the Lamb, I will sing, I will sing,
to God and to the Lamb, I will sing.
To God and to the Lamb who is the great I AM,
while millions join the theme, I will sing, I will sing,
while millions join the theme I will sing.

And when from death I'm free, I'll sing on, I'll sing on,
and when from death I'm free, I'll sing on.
And when from death I'm free I'll sing and joyful be,
and through eternity I'll sing on, I'll sing on,
and through eternity I'll sing on.   American folk hymn

B RETHREN," the minister said in a harsh whisper, without moving.

"Yes, Jesus!" the woman's voice said, hushed yet.

"Breddren en sistuhn!" His voice rang again, with the horns. He removed his arm and stood erect and raised his hands. "I got de ricklickshun en de blood of de Lamb!" They did not mark just when his intonation, his pronunciation, became negroid, they just sat swaying a little in their seats as the voice took them into itself.

"When de long, cold—Oh, I tells you, breddren, when de long, cold—I sees de light en I sees de word, po sinner! Dey passed away in Egypt, de swingin chariots; de generations passed away. Wus a rich man: whar he now, O breddren? Wus a po man: whar he now, O sistuhn? Oh I tells you, ef you aint got de milk en de dew of de old salvation when de long, cold years rolls away!"

"Yes, Jesus!"

"I tells you, breddren, en I tells you, sistuhn, dey'll come a time. Po sinner sayin Let me lay down wid de Lawd, lemme lay down my load. Den whut Jesus gwine say, O breddren? O sistuhn? Is you got de ricklickshun en de blood of de Lamb? Case I aint gwine load down heaven!"

He fumbled in his coat and took out a handkerchief and mopped his face. A low concerted sound rose from the congregation: "Mmmmmmmmmmmmmm!" The woman's voice said, "Yes, Jesus! Jesus!"

"Breddren! Look at dem little chillen settin dar. Jesus wus like dat once. He mammy suffered de glory en de pangs. Sometime maybe she helt him at de nightfall, whilst de angels singin him to sleep; maybe she look out de do' en see de Roman po-lice passin." He tramped back and forth, mopping his face. "Listen, breddren! I sees de day. Ma'y settin in de do' wid Jesus on her lap, de little Jesus. Like dem chillen dar, de little Jesus. I hears de angels singin de peaceful songs en de glory; I sees de closin eyes; sees Mary jump up, sees de sojer face: We gwine to kill! We gwine to kill! We gwine to kill yo little Jesus! I hears de weepin en de lamentation of de po mammy widout de salvation en de word of God!"

"Mmmmmmmmmmmmmmmmmm! Jesus! Little Jesus!" and another voice, rising: "I sees, O Jesus! Oh I sees!" and still another, without words, like bubbles rising in water.

"I sees hit, breddren! I sees hit! Sees de blastin, blindin sight! I sees Calvary, wid de sacred trees, sees de thief en de murderer en de least of dese; I hears de boasting en de braggin: Ef you be Jesus, lif up yo tree en walk! I hears de wailin of women en de evenin lamentations; I hears de weepin en de cryin en de turnt-away face of God: dey done kilt Jesus; dey done kilt my Son!"

"Mmmmmmmmmmmmmmmm. Jesus! I sees, O Jesus!"

"O blind sinner! Breddren, I tells you; sistuhn, I says to you, when de Lawd did turn His mighty face, say, Aint gwine overload heaven! I can see de widowed God shet His do'; I sees de whelmin flood roll between; I sees de darkness en de death everlastin upon de generations. Den, lo! Breddren! Yes, breddren! Whut I see? Whut I see, O sinner? I sees de resurrection en de light; sees de meek Jesus sayin Dey kilt Me dat ye shall live again; I died dat dem whut sees en believes shall never die. Breddren, O breddren! I sees de doom crack en hears de golden horns shoutin down de glory, en de arisen dead whut got de blood en de ricklickshun of de Lamb!"

In the midst of the voices and the hands Ben sat, rapt in his sweet blue gaze. Dilsey sat bolt upright beside, crying rigidly and quietly in the annealment and the blood of the remembered Lamb.

As they walked through the bright noon, up the sandy road with the dispersing congregation talking easily again group to group, she continued to weep, unmindful of the talk.

"He sho a preacher, mon! He didn't look like much at first, but hush!"

"He seed de power en de glory."

"Yes, suh. He seed hit. Face to face he seed hit."

Dilsey made no sound, her face did not quiver as the tears took their sunken and devious courses, walking with her head up, making no effort to dry them away even.

"Whyn't you quit dat, mammy?" Frony said, "Wid all dese people lookin. We be passin white folks soon."

"I've seed de first en de last," Dilsey said. "Never you mind me."

"First en last whut?" Frony said.

"Never you mind," Dilsey said. "I seed de beginnin, en now I sees de endin."   William Faulkner

A T the Lamb's high feast we sing
Praise to our victorious king,
Who has washed us in the tide
Flowing from his pierced side.

Praise we him, whose love divine
Gives his sacred blood for wine,
Gives his body for the feast,
Christ the victim, Christ the priest.

Where the paschal blood is poured,
Death's dark angel sheathes his sword;
Israel's hosts triumphant go
Through the wave that drowns the foe.

Praise we Christ, whose blood was shed,
Paschal victim, paschal bread;
With sincerity and love
Eat we manna from above.

Now no more can death appall,
Now no more the grave enthrall;
You have opened paradise,
Fourth century hymn   And in you your saints shall rise.

DAY 13

Y OU must wash each other's feet.

B EFORE the feast of Passover, Jesus knew that his hour had
come to pass from this world to the Father. He loved his
own in the world and he loved them to the end. The devil
had already induced Judas, son of Simon the Iscariot, to
hand him over. So, during supper, fully aware that the Father
had put everything into his power and that he had come from
God and was returning to God, he rose from supper and took
off his outer garments. He took a towel and tied it around his
waist. Then he poured water into a basin and began to wash
the disciples' feet and dry them with the towel around his
waist.   John 13:1–5

L ET us come to the gospel of God. I find the Lord divesting
himself of his garments, and girding himself with a
towel, pouring water into a basin, washing the feet of his
disciples. This water was that heavenly dew; this was proph-
esied: that the Lord Jesus would wash the feet of his disciples
with that heavenly dew. And now let the feet of our souls be
extended. The Lord Jesus wishes to wash our feet also, for
not to Peter alone but to each one of the faithful does he say:
"If I wash not thy feet, thou shalt have no part with me."

Therefore, Lord Jesus, let this water come into my soul, into
my flesh, that by the moisture of this rain the valleys of our
minds and the fields of our inmost hearts may grow green.
Let your drops come upon me, besprinkling grace and
immortality. Wash the steps of my mind, that I may not sin   Ambrose
again.   Fourth century

B ECAUSE we have been gifted with God's peace in the
risen Christ, we are called to our own peace and to the
making of peace in our world. As disciples and as children of
God it is our task to seek for ways in which to make the
forgiveness, justice and mercy and love of God visible in a
world where violence and enmity are too often the norm.   Challenge of Peace

L ORD God, your love has called us here
as we, by love, for love were made.
Your living likeness still we bear,
though marred, dishonored, disobeyed.
  We come, with all our heart and mind
  your call to hear, your love to find.

We come with self-inflicted pains
of broken trust and chosen wrong,
half-free, half-bound by inner chains,
by social forces swept along,
  by powers and systems close confined
  yet seeking hope for humankind.

Lord God, in Christ you call our name
and then receive us as your own
not through some merit, right or claim
but by your gracious love alone.
  We strain to glimpse your mercy seat
  and find you kneeling at our feet.

Then take the towel, and break the bread,
and humble us, and call us friends.
Suffer and serve till all are fed
and show how grandly love intends
  to work till all creation sings,
  to fill all worlds, to crown all things.

Lord God, in Christ you set us free
your life to live, your joy to share.
Give us your Spirit's liberty
to turn from guilt and dull despair
  and offer all that faith can do
Brian Wren   while love is making all things new.

F OR my head is wet with dew,
my locks with the moisture of the night.
I have taken off my robe,
am I then to put it on?
I have bathed my feet,
am I then to soil them?   Song of Songs 5:2–3

A Christian is a perfectly free lord of all, subject to
none.
A Christian is a perfectly dutiful servant of all, subject
to all.   Martin Luther
                                                           Sixteenth century

DAY 14

Y OU crushed the heads of Leviathan,
and made food of him for the dolphins.

O N that day,
will the LORD punish with a sword
which is hard and great and strong,
Leviathan the fleeing serpent,
Leviathan the coiled serpent;
and the LORD will slay the dragon that is in the sea.   Isaiah 27:1

C AN you lead about Leviathan with a hook,
  or curb his tongue with a bit?
Can you put a rope into his nose,
  or pierce through his cheek with a gaff?
Will he then plead with you, time after time,
  or address you with tender words?
Will he make an agreement with you
  that you may have him as a slave forever?
Can you play with him as with a bird?
  Can you put him in leash for your maidens?
Will the traders bargain for him?
  Will the merchants divide him up?
Can you fill his hide with barbs,
  or his head with fish spears?
Once you but lay a hand upon him,
  no need to recall any other conflict!
Is he not relentless when aroused;
  who then dares stand before him?
Whoever might vainly hope to do so
  need only see him to be overthrown.
Who has assailed him and come off safe—
  Who under all the heavens?
I need hardly mention his limbs,
  his strength, and the fitness of his armor.
Who can strip off his outer garment,
  or penetrate his double corselet?
Who can force open the doors of his mouth,
  close to his terrible teeth?
Rows of scales are on his back,
  tightly sealed together;
They are fitted each so close to the next
  that no space intervenes;
So joined one to another

that they hold fast and cannot be parted.
When he sneezes, light flashes forth;
  his eyes are like those of the dawn.
Out of his mouth go forth firebrands;
  sparks of fire leap forth.
From his nostrils issues steam,
  as from a seething pot or bowl.
His breath sets coals afire;
  a flame pours from his mouth.
Strength abides in his neck,
  and terror leaps before him.
His heart is hard as stone:
  his flesh, as the lower millstone.
When he rises up, the mighty are afraid;
  the waves of the sea fall back.
Should the sword reach him, it will not avail;
  nor will the spear, nor the dart, nor the javelin.
He regards iron as straw,
  and bronze as rotten wood.
The arrow will not put him to flight;
  slingstones used against him are but straws.
Clubs he esteems as splinters;
  he laughs at the crash of the spear.
His belly is sharp as pottery fragments;
  he spreads like a threshing sledge upon the mire.
He makes the depths boil like a pot;
  the sea he churns like perfume in a kettle.
Behind him he leaves a shining path;
  you would think the deep had the hoary head of age.
Upon the earth there is not his like,
  intrepid he was made.
All, however lofty, fear him;
  he is king over all proud beasts.   Job 40:25—41:26

THE Holy One, blessed be he, will in time to come make a banquet for the righteous from the flesh of Leviathan. The rest of Leviathan will be distributed and sold in the markets of Jerusalem. The Holy One, blessed be he, will in time to come make a tabernacle for the righteous from the skin of Leviathan. . . . The rest of Leviathan will be spread by the Holy One, blessed be he, upon the walls of Jerusalem, and its splendour will shine from one end of the world to the other; as it is said: "And nations shall walk at thy light, and kings at the brightness of thy rising."

Rabbinic legend

WE should keep before our minds the dramatic meaning of the Easter night as a struggle with the demon. Cyril of Jerusalem shows us that the descent into the baptismal pool is, as it were, a descent into the waters of death which are the dwelling place of the dragon of the sea, as Christ went down into the Jordan to crush the power of the dragon who was hidden there: "The dragon Leviathan, according to Job," writes Cyril, "was in the waters, and was taking the Jordan into his gullet. But, as the heads of the dragon had to be crushed, Jesus, having descended into the waters, chained fast the strong one."

Jean Danielou

WHILE they were still incredulous for joy and were amazed, he asked them, "Have you anything here to eat?" They gave him a piece of baked fish; he took it and ate it in front of them.

Luke 24:41–43

A FTER this, Jesus revealed himself again to his disciples at the Sea of Tiberias. He revealed himself in this way. Together were Simon Peter, Thomas called Didymus, Nathanael from Cana in Galilee, Zebedee's sons, and two others of his disciples. Simon Peter said to them, "I am going fishing." They said to him, "We also will come with you." So they went out and got into the boat, but that night they caught nothing. When it was already dawn, Jesus was standing on the shore; but the disciples did not realize that it was Jesus. Jesus said to them, "Children, have you caught anything to eat?" They answered him, "No." So he said to them, "Cast the net over the right side of the boat and you will find something." So they cast it, and were not able to pull it in because of the number of fish. So the disciple whom Jesus loved said to Peter, "It is the Lord." When Simon Peter heard that it was the Lord, he tucked in his garment, for he was lightly clad, and jumped into the sea. The other disciples came in the boat, for they were not far from shore, only about a hundred yards, dragging the net with the fish. When they climbed out on shore, they saw a charcoal fire with fish on it and bread. Jesus said to them, "Bring some of the fish you just caught." So Simon Peter went over and dragged the net ashore full of one hundred fifty-three large fish. Even though there were so many, the net was not torn. Jesus said to them, "Come have breakfast." And none of the disciples dared to ask him, "Who are you?" because they realized it was the Lord. Jesus came over and took the bread and gave it to them, and in like manner the fish. This was now the third time Jesus was revealed to his disciples after being raised from the dead.   John 21:1–14

ICHTHUS-BORN, divine children of a heavenly father,
drink with heartfelt reverence God's waters,
  the source of immortality to mortals.
Fortify your soul, friend, with the ever-flowing waters
    of wisdom, the enriching.
Take the honey-sweet food he offers
    who saves the saints;
    eat as a hungry man eats
    of the Ichthus you hold in your hands.
Feed us then, Lord; Saviour, feed us, I pray,
    with the Ichthus.

Ichthus: Fish (Greek)
Pectorius of Autun
Third century

THERE were those who thought that the menu of the great
meal of the day of God would be Leviathan, served up as
a shining supper. Perhaps that very idea echoes on the edges
of the stories of the fish meal served by Jesus in the wilderness or of the resurrection appearance at the fish breakfast.
But there may be an even deeper resonance among Christians. Christ himself is the fish. And the eucharist is the
foretaste of that great meal. It is eating the death and terror
and chaos which are gathered into Christ's cross, now cut up
and peacefully ordered into love.

Some scholars even think that the old practice of eating a fish
meal on Friday night (on the Sabbath) originally meant to
recall the hope for the meal of the day of God. No wonder
that Christians continue to eat fish on Friday, the day that
they believed Leviathan was caught and cut up.

Gordon Lathrop

DEATH is swallowed up in victory.
Where, O death, is your victory?
Where, O death, is your sting?

1 Corinthians
15:54–55
Hosea 13:14

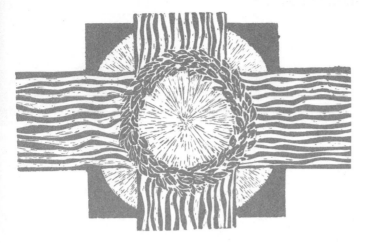

THIRD
WEEK
OF
EASTER

THEN God said to Noah: "Go out of the ark, you and all your household."

MAKE yourself an ark of gopherwood, put various compartments in it, and cover it inside and out with pitch. This is how you shall build it: the length of the ark shall be three hundred cubits, its width fifty cubits, and its height thirty cubits. Make an opening for daylight in the ark, and finish the ark a cubit above it. Put an entrance in the side of the ark, which you shall make with bottom, second and third decks. I, on my part, am about to bring the flood waters on the earth, to destroy everywhere all creatures in which there is the breath of life; everything on earth shall perish.

Genesis 6:14–17

WE turn to you for protection,
holy Mother of God.
Listen to our prayers
and help us in our needs.
Save us from every danger,
glorious and blessed Virgin.

Third century prayer

Robert Stephen
Hawker
Nineteenth century

T HE ark, that womb of second birth . . .

A LTHOUGH the winds be mighty,
And high waves in the sea,
Yet Wisdom is the pilot—
The powerful Lord is he;
Despite transgression's deluge,
Corruptions foul and dark,
We'll yet escape the drowning
Ann Griffiths
Eighteenth century
Because God is our ark.

DAY 16

J ESUS sent them out two by two.

O N the precise day named, Noah and his sons Shem,
Ham and Japheth, and Noah's wife, and the three
wives of Noah's sons had entered the ark, together with
every kind of wild beast, every kind of domestic animal,
every kind of creeping thing of the earth, and every kind of
bird. Pairs of all creatures in which there was the breath of
life entered the ark with Noah. Those that entered were male
and female, and of all species they came, as God had
Genesis 7:13–16   commanded Noah. Then the LORD shut him in.

A GAIN I say to you, if two of you agree on earth about
anything for which they are to pray, it shall be granted

to them by my heavenly Father. For where two or three are gathered together in my name, there am I in the midst of them.

Matthew 18:19–20

H E is the Way.
Follow Him through the Land of Unlikeness,
You will see rare beasts, and have unique adventures.
He is the Truth.
Seek Him in the Kingdom of Anxiety;
You will come to a great city that has expected your return
    for years.
He is the Life!
Love Him in the World of the Flesh;
And at your marriage all its occasions shall dance for joy.

W. H. Auden

Day 17

L ET not the flood-waters overwhelm me, nor the abyss swallow me up.

T HE flood continued upon the earth for forty days. As the waters increased, they lifted the ark, so that it rose above the earth. The swelling waters increased greatly, but the ark floated on the surface of the waters.

Genesis 7:17–18

F RESH from the heavenly stream again the sheep
receive their mark from Christ the Shepherd's
    hand.
O water-born, go where the Spirit calls:
    seek unity, and all his gifts are yours.
You who have taken up the cross, avoid the tempests of
    the world: so bids this place.

Consignatorium
inscription
Fifth century

THIS joyful Eastertide, away with sin and sorrow!
Our Love, the Crucified, hath sprung to life this
    morrow.
Had Christ, that once was slain, ne'er burst his three-day
    prison,
our faith had been in vain;
    but now is Christ arisen, arisen, arisen!
But now is Christ arisen!

Death's flood hath lost its chill, since Jesus crossed the
    river:
Lord of all life, from ill our passing life deliver,
Had Christ, that once was slain, ne'er burst his three-day
    prison,
our faith had been in vain;
    but now is Christ arisen, arisen, arisen!
But now is Christ arisen!

Our flesh in hope shall rest, and for a season slumber,
till trump from east to west shall wake the dead in
    number.
Had Christ, that once was slain, ne'er burst his three-day
    prison,
our faith had been in vain;
    but now is Christ arisen, arisen, arisen!
George Ratcliffe
Woodward   But now is Christ arisen!

IN the same instant you died and were born again; the
saving water was both your tomb and your mother.

Solomon's phrase in another context is very apposite here.
He spoke of a time to give birth, and a time to die. For you,
however, it was the reverse: a time to die, and a time to be
Cyril of Jerusalem   born, although in fact both events took place at the same
Fourth century   time and your birth was simultaneous with your death.

B UT now, thus says the LORD,
who created you, O Jacob, and formed you,
    O Israel:
Fear not, for I have redeemed you;
    I have called you by name: you are mine.
When you pass through the water, I will be with you;
    in the rivers you shall not drown.
When you walk through fire, you shall not be burned;
    the flames shall not consume you.
For I am the LORD, your God,
    the Holy One of Israel, your savior.   Isaiah 43:1–3

T EMPTATION is like a winter torrent difficult to cross. Some
then, being most skillful swimmers, pass over, not being
whelmed beneath temptations, nor swept down by them at
all; while others who are not such, entering into them, sink
in them. As for example, Judas entering into the temptation
of covetousness, swam not through it, but sinking beneath it,
was choked both in body and spirit. Peter entered into the
temptation of the denial; but having entered it, he was not
overwhelmed by it, but strongly swimming through it, he   Cyril of Jerusalem
was delivered from the temptation.   Fourth century

H E would let the world do its will and thereby accom-
plish the will of the Father; he would grant the world its
will, thereby breaking the world's will; he would allow his
own vessel to be shattered, thereby pouring himself out; but
pouring out one single drop of the divine Heart's blood he
would sweeten the immense and bitter ocean. This was
intended to be the most incomprehensible of exchanges:
from the most extreme opposition would come the highest
union, and the might of his supreme victory was to prove
itself in his utter disgrace and defeat. For his weakness would

already be the victory of his love for the Father, reconciliation in the eyes of the Father, and, as a deed of his supreme strength, this weakness would be so great that it would far surpass and sustain in itself the world's pitiful feebleness. He alone would henceforth be the measure and thus also the meaning of all impotence. He wanted to sink so low that in the future all falling would be a falling into him, and every streamlet of bitterness and despair would henceforth run down into his lowermost abyss.

Hans Urs von
Balthasar

DAY 18

T HE song of the dove is heard in our land.

T HEN he sent out a dove, to see if the waters had lessened on the earth. But the dove could find no place to alight and perch, and it returned to him in the ark, for there was water all over the earth. Putting out his hand, he caught the dove and drew it back to him inside the ark. He waited seven days more and again sent the dove out from the ark.

Genesis 8:8–10

F OR just as, after the waters of the deluge, by which the old iniquity was purged—after the baptism, so to say, of the world—a dove was the herald which announced to the earth the assuagement of celestial wrath, when she had been sent her way out of the ark, and had returned with the olive branch, a sign which even among the nations is the foretoken of peace; so by the self-same law of heavenly effect, to earth—that is, to our flesh—as it emerges from the font, flies the dove of the Holy Spirit, bringing us the peace of God sent out from the heavens.

Tertullian
Third century

B UT the LORD sent a large fish, that swallowed Jonah [Editor's note: In Hebrew, "jonah" means "dove"]; and he remained in the belly of the fish three days and three nights. From the belly of the fish Jonah said this prayer to the LORD, his God:

The waters swirled about me, threatening my life;
> the abyss enveloped me;
> seaweed clung about my head.
Down I went to the roots of the mountains;
> the bars of the nether world
> were closing behind me forever,
But you brought up my life from the pit,
> O LORD, my God.

Then the LORD commanded the fish to spew Jonah upon the shore.

Jonah 2:1–2, 6–7, 11

I T happened in those days that Jesus came from Nazareth of Galilee and was baptized in the Jordan by John. On coming up out of the water he saw the heavens being torn open and the Spirit, like a dove, descending upon him.

Mark 1:9–10

R ISE, therefore, beloved of Christ, be like the dove that makes its nest in the heights in the mouth of a cleft. There, like a sparrow that finds a home, do not cease to keep watch; there, like the turtledove, hide the offsprings of your chaste love. There, apply your mouth to draw water from the Savior's fountains for this is the river arising from the midst of paradise which, divided into four branches and flowing into devout hearts, waters and makes fertile the whole earth.

Bonaventure
Thirteenth century

W HILST thou didst act so lovingly towards me, and didst not cease to draw my soul from vanity and to thyself, it happened on a certain day, between the Festival of the Resurrection and Ascension, that I went into the court before Prime, and seated myself near the fountain,—and I began to consider the beauty of the place, which charmed me on account of the clear and flowing stream, the verdure of the trees which surrounded it, and the flight of the birds, and particularly of the doves,—above all, the sweet calm,—apart from all, and considering within myself what would make this place most useful to me, I thought that it would be the friendship of a wise and intimate companion, who would sweeten my solitude or render it useful to others, when thou, my Lord and my God who are a torrent of inestimable pleasure, after having inspired me with the first impulse of this desire, thou didst will to be also the end of it, inspiring me with the thought that if by continual gratitude I return thy graces to thee, as a stream returns to its source; if, increasing in the love of virtue, I put forth, like the trees, the flowers of good works; furthermore, if, despising the things of earth, I fly upwards, freely, like the birds, and thus free my senses from the distraction of exterior things,—my soul would then be empty, and my heart would be an agreeable abode for thee.

Gertrude the Great
Thirteenth century

DAY 19

L IKE a green olive tree in the house of God, I trust in the kindness of God.

I N the evening the dove came back to him, and there in its bill was a plucked-off olive leaf! So Noah knew that the waters had lessened on the earth.

Genesis 8:11

THEN, when you were stripped, you were anointed with exorcized oil, from the very hairs of your head to your feet, and were made partakers of the good olive tree, Jesus Christ.

Cyril of Jerusalem
Fourth century

THANKS be to God, who unfailingly leads us on in Christ's triumphal train, and employs us to diffuse the fragrance of his knowledge everywhere! We are an aroma of Christ for God's sake, both among those who are being saved and those on the way to destruction; to the latter an odor dealing death, to the former a breath bringing life.

2 Corinthians 2:14–16

THE sign of Christ is traced on the part of the body that is most immediately visible to anyone who meets us. Nothing is more difficult for us to hide than that which is in any way written on our forehead. Anyone who has ever had to wear even a small bandaid on the forehead after a mishap can attest to the truth of what I am saying. . . .

Chrism is produced by adding aromatic essences (especially balsam) to olive oil. Here again the element of public manifestation that is proper to confirmation exercises its influence. Paul says of Christians that they should be "the aroma of Christ" (2 Corinthians 2:14). Wherever Christians live their baptism and confirmation in an authentic way, they emit as it were a "strong and wholesome fragrance."

How can anyone observe Mother Teresa at work serving the starving children of Calcutta and not smell something of this strong and wholesome fragrance, this "aroma of Christ"? This woman has translated into action what the bishop meant when on the day of her confirmation he laid his hand on her head and anointed her forehead so that she might confess her faith and bear witness to it.

Balthasar Fischer

M ARY sings,
"Suddenly sorrow has been changed to joy,
And all has become joyous and a cause for rejoicing;
I do not hesitate to say, 'I have been glorified as Moses,'
For I have seen, I have seen—not on the mountain but in
   the tomb,
Not concealed by a cloud, but by flesh,
The Lord of the Immortals and of the clouds,
Lord of old, now and forever;
And he said, 'Mary, hasten and tell
Those who love me that I have arisen;
Take me on your tongue, like a branch of the olive.
To the descendants of Noah, announce the good news,
Pointing out to them that death is destroyed and that he
   has arisen,
He who offers resurrection to the fallen.' "

Romanos
Sixth century

L ET us therefore bear fruit as we should!
Let our fate be not that of the barren fig tree;
let Jesus not come again today
to curse it for its barrenness!

May we all say: "As for me,
like a green olive tree in the house of God,
I have forever put my hope in the mercy of God!"
An olive tree that is not material
but spiritual, a bearer of light.

It is for God, then, to plant and water
but for you to bear fruit;
for God to give his grace
but for you to receive and preserve it.

Cyril of Jerusalem
Fourth century

A H, how good and lovely it is
For brothers and sisters to live in community!
Like fragrant oil upon one's head
    Flowing down one's beard,
The beard of Aaron, flowing down
    The collar of his robes;
Like the dew of Mount Hermon, coming down
    Upon the hills of Zion—
There the Lord confers the blessing,
    Life that lasts forever.   Psalm 133

DAY 20

T HEN I saw a new heaven and a new earth.

I N the second month, on the twenty-seventh day of the
month, the earth was dry. Then God said to Noah: "Go out
of the ark, together with your wife and your sons and your
sons' wives. Bring out with you every living thing that is with
you—all bodily creatures, be they birds or animals or
creeping things of the earth—and let them abound on the
earth, breeding and multiplying on it." So Noah came out,
together with his wife and his sons and his sons' wives; and
all the animals, wild and tame, all the birds, and all the
creeping creatures of the earth left the ark, one kind after
another.   Genesis 8:14–19

THOUGH nature's strength decay,
And earth and hell withstand,
To Canaan's bounds I urge my way
At his command.
The watery deep I pass,
With Jesus in my view,
And through the howling wilderness
My way pursue.

The goodly land I see,
With peace and plenty blest;
A land of sacred liberty,
And endless rest.
There milk and honey flow,
And oil and wine abound,
And trees of life forever grow
With mercy crowned.

Thomas Olivers
Eighteenth century

O thou whose pow'r o'er moving worlds presides,
Whose voice created, and whose wisdom guides,
On darkling man in pure effulgence shine,
And clear the clouded mind with light divine.
'Tis thine alone to calm the pious breast
With silent confidence and holy rest:
From thee, great God, we spring, to thee we tend,
Path, motive, guide, original, and end.

Boethius
Sixth century

L O, I am about to create new heavens
and a new earth;
The things of the past shall not be remembered
or come to mind.
Instead, there shall always be rejoicing and happiness
in what I create;
For I create Jerusalem to be a joy and its people
to be a delight;
I will rejoice in Jerusalem
and exult in my people.
No longer shall the sound of weeping be heard there,
or the sound of crying;
No longer shall there be in it
an infant who lives but a few days,
or an old man who does not round out his full lifetime;
He dies a mere youth who reaches but a hundred years,
and he who fails of a hundred shall be thought
accursed.
They shall live in the houses they build,
and eat the fruit of the vineyards they plant;
They shall not build houses for others to live in,
or plant for others to eat.
As the years of a tree, so the years of my people;
and my chosen ones shall long enjoy
the produce of their hands.
They shall not toil in vain,
nor beget children for sudden destruction;
For a race blessed by the LORD are they
and their offspring.
Before they call, I will answer;
while they are yet speaking, I will hearken to them.   Isaiah 65:17–25

C HRISTIAN communities that commit themselves to soli-
darity with those suffering and to confrontation with
those attitudes and ways of acting which institutionalize
injustice, will themselves experience the power and presence of Christ. They will embody in their lives the values of
the new creation while they labor under the old. The quest
for economic and social justice will always combine hope
and realism, and must be renewed by every generation. It
involves diagnosing those situations that continue to alien-
ate the world from God's creative love as well as presenting
hopeful alternatives that arise from living in a renewed
creation. This quest arises from faith and is sustained by
Economic Justice   hope as it seeks to speak to a broken world of God's justice
for All   and loving kindness.

A LL these died in faith. They did not receive what had
been promised but saw it and greeted it from afar and
acknowledged themselves to be strangers and aliens on
earth, for those who speak thus show that they are seeking a
homeland. If they had been thinking of the land from which
they had come, they would have had opportunity to return.
Hebrews 11:13–16   But now they desire a better homeland, a heavenly one.

DAY 21

A ROUND the throne was a rainbow as brilliant as
emerald.

G OD said to Noah and to his sons with him: "See, I am now establishing my covenant with you and your descendants after you and with every living creature that was with you: all the birds, and the various tame and wild animals that were with you and came out of the ark. I will establish my covenant with you, that never again shall all bodily creatures be destroyed by the waters of a flood; there shall not be another flood to devastate the earth." God added: "This is the sign that I am giving for all ages to come, of the covenant between me and you and every living creature with you: I set my bow in the clouds to serve as a sign of the covenant between me and the earth. When I bring clouds over the earth, and the bow appears in the clouds, I will recall the covenant I have made between me and you and all living beings, so that the waters shall never again become a flood to destroy all mortal beings. As the bow appears in the clouds, I will see it and recall the everlasting covenant that I have established between God and all living beings—all mortal creatures that are on earth."

Genesis 9:8–16

T HROUGHOUT Easter's fifty days the paschal candle stands, prominent and lofty, in the middle of the eucharistic hall. As the center pole of the new creation, the candle is Christ, the Alpha and Omega of all times and ages. Five wax nails are inserted into the candle to signify the wounds that Jesus received in his hands, feet and side when he was crucified. "By his holy and glorious wounds, may Christ our Lord guard and keep us." These wounds do not vanish. They remain with Jesus who repeatedly shows them to his disciples. They are offered as marks of recognition: "Look at my hands and my feet; it is really I." (Luke 24:39)

Lit as the first act of the community's paschal watch, this mighty pillar of light remains in place for the duration of the fifty days enabling the faithful to see, to recognize, to find their way. It is the light of Christ revealing the love of the Father, and the power of the Spirit in whom humanity is born from above.

Patrick Regan

NOAH, Noah, here I behest [pledge] thee a hest
That man, woman, fowl and beast
With water, while this world shall last
  I will no more spill.

My bow between you and me
  In the firmament shall be
By very token that you shall see
  That such vengeance shall cease.

Where clouds in the welkin [heavens] been
  That ev'ry bow shall be seen
In token that my wrath and teen [grief]
  Shall never thus wreaked be.

The string is turned towards you
  And toward me is bent the bow
That such weather shall never show
  And this behight [promise] I thee.

My blessings, Noah, I give thee here
  To thee, Noah, my servant dear,
For vengeance shall no more appear;
  And now, farewell, my darling dear.

Chester miracle play
Sixteenth century

YEA, Truth and Justice then
  Will down return to men,
  Orb'd in a rainbow; and like glories wearing
Mercy will sit between,
Thron'd in celestial sheen,
  With radiant feet the tissu'd clouds down steering;
And Heav'n as at some festival
Will open wide the gates of her high palace hall.

John Milton
Seventeenth century

FOURTH WEEK OF EASTER

T ELL me, you whom my heart loves, where you pasture your flock.

W HAT are the pastures of these sheep if they are not the deepest joys of the everlasting fresh pastures of paradise? For the pasture of the saints is to see God face to face; when the vision of God never fails, the soul receives its fill of the food of life for ever. And so, dear brothers and sisters, let us seek these pastures and there join in the joy of the celebrations of so many citizens of heaven. Let their happiness and rejoicing be an invitation to us. Let our hearts grow warm, let our faith be rekindled, let our desires for heavenly things grow warm; for to love like this is to be on the way.

Gregory the Great
Sixth century

THIS sheep that bleats in hunger, who implores a pasturage capable of fattening her, is the faithful soul who wishes to remain with Christ who is her proper pasture. She wants to go where there is new grass, and just wants to gather the flowers, and contemplate the beauty of her delightful love, and with a great desire of her heart she wants to fill her breasts again with the milk of charity, and enter into the garden of her true love, and gather red roses, and pick white roses, and drink in the passion of that white lamb, pure in sacrifice, who for our sins was lifted up onto the cross. Behold then the sheep with the immaculate lamb, behold the faithful soul with Christ, who is glad of that love, who desires it so much that he is always famished and can never be sated by it, for too little does he find of that milk of love.

Umilta of Faenza
Thirteenth century

SPRING has now unwrapped the flow'rs;
Day is fast reviving.
Life in all its fertile pow'rs
Toward the light is striving.
Herb and plant that winter-long
    Slumbered at their leisure,
Now bestirring green and strong
Find in growth their pleasure!

All the world has come alive.
    All the earth is budding.
Bees are humming round the hive,
Done with winter's brooding.
Snow and frost have been undone.
    Winds are soft and tender.
High above the regal sun
Shines in all its splendor!

This our joy and this our feast,
    This our great surprising:

Young and old and best and least
See their own arising.
We, the newborn patterns are
    Of our God and Maker:
Christ, our spring beyond compare!
Christ, our good creator!

Easter carol
Sixteenth century

L ITTLE Lamb, who made thee?
    Dost thou know who made thee?
Gave thee life, and bid thee feed
By the stream and o'er the mead;
Gave thee clothing of delight,
Softest clothing, wooly, bright;
Gave thee such a tender voice,
Making all the vales rejoice?
    Little Lamb, who made thee?
    Dost thou know who made thee?

Little Lamb, I'll tell thee,
    Little Lamb, I'll tell thee:
He is called by thy name,
For he calls himself a Lamb.
He is meek, and he is mild;
He became a little child.
I a child, and thou a lamb,
We are called by his name.
    Little Lamb, God bless thee!
    Little Lamb, God bless thee!

William Blake
Eighteenth century

Y OU have fed off their milk, worn their wool, and slaughtered the fatlings, but the sheep you have not pastured. You did not strengthen the weak nor heal the sick nor bind up the injured. You did not bring back the strayed nor seek the lost, but you lorded it over them harshly and brutally. So they were scattered for lack of a shepherd, and became food for all the wild beasts. My sheep were scattered and wandered over all the mountains and high hills; my sheep were scattered over the whole earth, with no one to look after them or to search for them.

For thus says the Lord God: I myself will look after and tend my sheep. In good pastures will I pasture them, and on the mountain heights of Israel shall be their grazing ground. There they shall lie down on good grazing ground, and in rich pastures shall they be pastured on the mountains of Israel. I myself will pasture my sheep; I myself will give them rest, says the Lord God. The lost I will seek out, the strayed I will bring back, the injured I will bind up, the sick I will heal, shepherding them rightly.

Ezekiel 34:3–6, 11, 14–16

DAY 23

I am the good shepherd.

T HE king of love my shepherd is,
Whose goodness fails me never;
I nothing lack if I am his,
And he is mine for ever.

Where streams of living water flow
My ransomed soul he's leading,

And where the verdant pastures grow
With food celestial feeding.

You spread a table in my sight;
Your saving grace bestowing;
And O what transport of delight
From your pure chalice flowing!

And so through all the length of days
Your goodness fails me never;
Good Shepherd, may I sing your praise
Within your house for ever.

Henry W. Baker
Nineteenth century

W HAT man among you having a hundred sheep and losing one of them would not leave the ninety-nine in the desert and go after the lost one until he finds it? And when he does find it, he sets it on his shoulders with great joy and, upon his arrival home, he calls together his friends and neighbors and says to them, "Rejoice with me because I have found my lost sheep." I tell you, in just the same way there will be more joy in heaven over one sinner who repents than over ninety-nine righteous people who have no need of repentance.

Luke 15:3–7

S HEPHERD of tender youth,
Guiding in love and truth through devious ways,
Christ, our triumphant king,
We come thy name to sing
And here our children bring to join thy praise.

Ever be thou our guide,
Our shepherd and our pride, our staff and song;
Jesus, thou Christ of God,
By thine enduring word
Lead us where thou hast trod, make our faith strong.

Clement of Alexandria
Third century

ONCE a young shepherd went off to despond:
how could he dance again? how could he sing?
All of his thoughts to his shepherdess cling,
with love in his heart like a ruinous wound.

The root of his sorrow? No, never the wound:
the lad was a lover and welcomed the dart
that lodged where it drank the red race of his heart—
but spurned by his fairest, went off to despond.

For only to think he was spurned, and by one
radiant shepherdess, drove him afar;
cost him a drubbing in foreigners' war,
with love in his heart like a ruinous wound.

The shepherd boy murmured: O murrain descend
on the traitor estranging my angel and me!
charming her vision that stares stonily
on the love in my heart like a ruinous wound.

Time passed: on a season he sprang from the ground,
swarmed a tall tree and arms balancing wide
beautifully grappled the tree till he died
of the love in his heart like a ruinous wound.

John of the Cross
Sixteenth century

HE said to him the third time, "Simon, son of John, do
you love me?" Peter was distressed that he had said to
him a third time, "Do you love me?" and he said to him,
"Lord, you know everything; you know that I love you."
John 21:17   Jesus said to him, "Feed my sheep."

F ROM your delightful stream you give them to drink.

THE wise are servants of the all-wise Master,
Legitimate child of a lawful Father;
  Famous army of the One who enlists soldiers,
    Jesus, our God;
Marvelous flock of a wonderful Shepherd,
  The field of the Farmer of all.
These are the waters of the ever-flowing stream,
  Divine shoots of a divine branch,
  Holy branches of a sacred root,
Like the beloved creature of the Creator of all creation,
  The very blessed senate of the undefiled Lord,
The disciples of Christ whom he himself, Savior of all,
    gathered together.
  He commanded them to live in life that knows
    no decay,
  As he bestows on them
  Glory from the heavens and an abundance of crowns.

Romanos
Sixth century

S HALL we gather at the river,
Where bright angel feet have trod;
With its crystal tide forever
Flowing by the throne of God?
Yes, we'll gather at the river,
The beautiful, the beautiful river;
Gather with the saints by the river
That flows by the throne of God.

Ere we reach the shining river,
Lay we ev'ry burden down;

Grace our spirits will deliver,
And provide a robe and crown.
Yes, we'll gather at the river,
The beautiful, the beautiful river;
Gather with the saints by the river

Robert Lowry
Nineteenth century

That flows by the throne of God.

A small cup held under a faucet
I collect what streams
from imagined hills?
How far the source
   first moisture
   on the earth's porous skin?
On the hand, a water-print;
in the mind, a twisting like a cold snake
   a thin river of words
   quivers and foams.

I drink
   I thirst
   drink bucketfuls
   torrents, lakes
   dream-waters rising
   from deep unconscious wells.
I drink and still thirst.

The river fills with swimming creatures
images, fish-populations, swarms
of pressing bodies.
It is the beginning of time:
I stand on the shore of a great astral sea.
Stars are copper pennies jingling in my pocket;
these waters are still

by which I stare into a night
wider, more luminous than the sun.

  I drink
but even as I lift it
bring it to my lips
the cup shatters: cold shards enter my life
slash like savage knives
the roots of my wishes.
  I thirst
with a pain I cannot hold.
And what am I:
  mere rising vapor
  no one can change?
  A water-charged mist
  no one can turn
  into the blessedness of flood?

Lord,
  I pull weight
  —bones and body—
  through the tortuous practice of a will seeking
not words cast in the shape of raindrops
not cupped signs to catch the melting snow
but
  the torrent of your eyes
  the streaming of your truth.

Lord, I thirst:
  disguised, an animal mask clamped
  over my face, I come with spirit-thirst
  to your shoreless flowing.
  I come by night
  to these dark unknown waters
  and lap the infinite freshness of you.   Catherine De Vinck

A s pants the hart for cooling streams
When heated in the chase,
So longs my soul, O God, for you
And your refreshing grace.

One trouble calls another on
And gathers overhead,
Falls splashing down, till round my soul
A rising sea is spread.

Why restless, why cast down, my soul?
Hope still, and you shall sing
Nahum Tate and The praise of him who is your God,
Nicholas Brady
Seventeenth century Your health's eternal spring.

Day 25

I am the sheepgate.

M ANY years ago I was traveling by donkey from
Nishapur, the city of the poet Omar Khayyam, in
eastern Iran to Sabsevar, a three days journey to the west. We
stopped in a tiny village of mud huts for the night, and when
we arose next morning the dry dusty land was covered with a
mantle of beautiful white snow.

As the donkey driver stated firmly that it was impossible for
his animals to move while the snow was so deep, there was
nothing to do but wait till the snow melted a bit. So all that
day we remained in the village.

In the afternoon I set out to see the sights about the village.
Not far away I came to a mound of earth piled up in a large

circle, like a crude rampart, and on the top of the mound all around the circle was a heap of dry thorns. As I stood wondering what this might be one of the villagers approached me. "Salaam," I said, "please tell me what this enclosure is for."

"Oh, that is for the sheep," he replied. "They are brought in here for the night for safety."

"Good," I said, "but why have the dry thorns been piled on top of the wall?"

"That," he replied. "is a protection against wolves. If a wolf tries to break in and attack the sheep, he will knock against the thorns, and they will make a noise, and the shepherd will wake up, and drive off the wolf."

"That is fine," I said, "but why does the wolf try to climb over the wall? Here is the entrance to the enclosure; it is open. There is no door to keep out the wolf; he could easily enter here."

"Oh no," said my guide, "you do not understand. That is where the shepherd sleeps, the shepherd is the door."

And then I understood something that had often puzzled me. It became clear to me why Jesus had in John 10 called himself first the Door and then immediately afterwards the Shepherd. Since he is the Shepherd he is also the Door.   Eric Bishop

I saw no temple in the city, for its temple is the Lord God almighty and the Lamb. The city had no need of sun or moon to shine on it, for the glory of God gave it light, and its lamp was the Lamb. The nations will walk by its light, and to it the kings of the earth will bring their treasure. During the day its gates will never be shut, and there will be no night there.   Revelation 21:22–25

B ECAUSE of sin
you would not enter into your glory
in the way your truth had intended.
Your garden was locked up,
and so we could not receive your fruits.
This is why you made the Word,
your only-begotten Son,
a gatekeeper.

O gentle gatekeeper!
O humble lamb!
You are the gardener,
and once you have opened the gate of the heavenly
garden,
paradise,
you offer us the flowers
and the fruits
of the eternal Godhead.

Catherine of Siena
Fourteenth century

DAY 26

T HE wolf and the lamb shall graze alike.

T HE fierce wolf came running with its mouth open toward
St. Francis.

The saint made the sign of the cross toward it. And the power
of God checked the wolf and made it slow down and close
its cruel mouth.

Then, calling to it, Francis said: "Come to me, Brother Wolf.
In the name of Christ, I order you not to hurt me or anyone."
It is marvelous to relate that as soon as he had made the sign

of the cross, the wolf closed its terrible jaws and stopped running, and as soon as he gave it that order, it lowered its head and lay down at the saint's feet, as though it had become a lamb.

And Francis said to it as it lay in front of him: "Brother Wolf, you have done great harm in this region, and you have committed horrible crimes by destroying God's creatures without any mercy. You have been destroying not only irrational animals, but you even have the more detestable brazenness to kill and devour human beings made in the image of God. . . . Consequently everyone is right in crying out against you and complaining, and this whole town is your enemy. But, Brother Wolf, I want to make peace between you and them, so that they will not be harmed by you any more, and after they have forgiven you all your past crimes, neither people nor dogs will pursue you any more."

The wolf showed by moving its body and tail and ears and by nodding its head that it willingly accepted what the saint had said and would observe it.

So Francis spoke again: "Brother Wolf, since you are willing to make and keep this peace pact, I promise you that I will have the people of this town give you food every day as long as you live, so that you will never again suffer from hunger, for I know that whatever evil you have been doing was done because of the urge of hunger. But, my Brother Wolf, since I am obtaining such a favor for you, I want you to promise me that you will never hurt any animal or human. Will you promise me that?"

The wolf gave a clear sign, by nodding its head, that it promised to do what the saint asked.

And Francis said: "Brother Wolf, I want you to give me a pledge so that I can confidently believe what you promise."

And as Francis held out his hand to receive the pledge, the wolf also raised its front paw and meekly and gently put it in Francis' hand as a sign that it was giving its pledge.

Then Francis said: "Brother Wolf, I order you, in the name of the Lord Jesus Christ, to come with me now, without fear, into the town to make this peace pact in the name of the Lord."

And the wolf immediately began to walk along beside Francis, just like a very gentle lamb. When the people saw this, they were greatly amazed, and the news spread quickly throughout the whole town, so that all of them, men as well as women, great and small, assembled on the market place, because Francis was there with the wolf.

From that day, the wolf and the people kept the pact which Francis made. The wolf lived two years more, and it went from door to door for food. It hurt no one, and no one hurt it. The people fed it courteously. And it is a striking fact that not a single dog ever barked at it.

The Little Flowers of St. Francis

B EHOLD, I am sending you like sheep in the midst of wolves; so be shrewd as serpents and simple as doves.

Matthew 10:16

I refuse to accept the idea that man is mere flotsam and jetsam in the river of life which surrounds him. I refuse to accept the view that mankind is so tragically bound to the starless midnight of racism and war that the bright daybreak of peace and brotherhood can never become a reality.

I refuse to accept the cynical notion that nation after nation must spiral down a militaristic stairway into the hell of thermonuclear destruction. I believe that unarmed truth and unconditional love will have the final word in reality. This is why right temporarily defeated is stronger than evil triumphant.

I believe that even amid today's mortar bursts and whining bullets, there is still hope for a brighter tomorrow. I believe that wounded justice, lying prostrate on the blood-flowing streets of our nations, can be lifted from this dust of shame to reign supreme among the children of men.

I have the audacity to believe that peoples everywhere can

have three meals a day for their bodies, education and culture for their minds, and dignity, equality and freedom for their spirits. I believe that what self-centered men have torn down, other-centered can build up. I still believe that one day mankind will bow before the altars of God and be crowned triumphant over war and bloodshed, and non-violent redemptive goodwill will proclaim the rule of the land. "And the lion and the lamb shall lie down together and every man shall sit under his own vine and fig tree and none shall be afraid." I still believe that we shall overcome.   Martin Luther King, Jr.

THEN the wolf shall be a guest of the lamb,
  and the leopard shall lie down with the kid;
The calf and the young lion shall browse together,
  with a little child to guide them.
The cow and the bear shall be neighbors,
  together their young shall rest;
  the lion shall eat hay like the ox.
The baby shall play by the cobra's den,
  and the child lay his hand on the adder's lair.
There shall be no harm or ruin on all my holy mountain;
  for the earth shall be filled with knowledge of the LORD,
  as water covers the sea.   Isaiah 11:6–9

THE supervisors and satraps went thronging to King Darius and said to him, "Did you not decree, O king, that no one is to address a petition to god or [mortal] for thirty days, except to you, O king; otherwise [that one] shall be cast into a den of lions?" The king answered them, "The decree is absolute, irrevocable under the Mede and Persian law." To this they replied, "Daniel, the Jewish exile, has paid no attention to you, O king, or to the decree you issued; three times a day he offers his prayer." The king was deeply grieved at this news and he made up his mind to save Daniel;

he worked till sunset to rescue him. But these men insisted. "Keep in mind, O king," they said, "that under the Mede and Persian law every royal prohibition or decree is irrevocable." So the king ordered Daniel to be brought and cast into the lions' den. To Daniel he said, "May your God, whom you serve so constantly, save you." To forestall any tampering, the king sealed with his own ring and the rings of the lords the stone that had been brought to block the opening of the den.

Then the king returned to his palace for the night; he refused to eat and he dismissed the entertainers. Since sleep was impossible for him, the king rose very early the next morning and hastened to the lions' den. As he drew near, he cried out to Daniel sorrowfully, "O Daniel, servant of the living God, has the God whom you serve so constantly been able to save you from the lions?" Daniel answered the king: "O king, live forever! My God has sent [an] angel and closed the lions' mouths so that they have not hurt me. For I have been found innocent before [God]; neither to you have I done any harm, O king!" This gave the king great joy. At his order Daniel was removed from the den, unhurt because he trusted in his

Daniel 6:7, 13–24   God.

Y E choirs of new Jerusalem,
  Your sweetest notes employ,
The paschal victory to hymn
  In strains of holy joy.

For Judah's Lion bursts his chains,
  Crushing the serpent's head;
And cries aloud through death's domains

Latin hymn
Eleventh century   To wake the imprison'd dead.

O NLY when the ram's horn resounds may they go up to the mountain.

W HEN they came to the place of which God had told him, Abraham built an altar there and arranged the wood on it. Next he tied up his son Isaac, and put him on top of the wood on the altar. Then he reached out and took the knife to slaughter his son. But the LORD'S messenger called to him from heaven, "Abraham, Abraham!" "Yes, Lord," he answered. "Do not lay your hand on the boy," said the messenger. "Do not do the least thing to him. I know now how devoted you are to God, since you did not withhold from me your own beloved son." As Abraham looked about, he spied a ram caught by its horns in the thicket. So he went and took the ram and offered it up as a holocaust in place of his son.

Genesis 22:9–13

T HE paschal lamb, like Isaac's ram,
in blood was offered for us,
pouring out his life that he
might to life restore us.

James Waring
McCrady

O N behalf of Isaac the righteous one, a ram appeared for slaughter, so that Isaac might be released from bonds. That ram, slain, ransomed Isaac; so also the Lord, slain, saved us, and bound, released us, and sacrificed, ransomed us.

And a little further on: For the Lord was a lamb like the ram which Abraham saw caught in a Sabek-tree. But the tree displayed the cross, and that place, Jerusalem, and the lamb, the Lord fettered for slaughter.

Of the same: "Caught by the horns" the Syriac and Hebrew

Melito of Sardis
Second century

express as "hanged," which prefigures in the plainest way the cross. But the word "ram" also makes this explicit: it did not say "a lamb," young like Isaac, but "a ram," full-grown like the Lord.

DAY 28

T HE Lamb on the throne will shepherd them.

L AMBS do not sit on thrones. Nor do they act as shepherds to the flock.

In Israel—and in the Near East generally—the tradition was indeed to call the kings and leaders of the people "shepherds" and thereby to call the people "flock."

But what is meant that the *lamb* is the shepherd? It is, of course, the truth about Jesus that is so spoken. He is made a weak and finally a slain man. A nothing. Yet this very one knows his own, calls them by name, will allow no snatching out of the flock. One who is no king at all is the only king. One who is no shepherd is the good shepherd for all the peoples.

It is the resurrection of the crucified one which is spoken by these images. In his "knowing us," that is his being in the midst of our agony, knowing it by sharing it, we are placed irrevocably in God's hand.

But how shall we know that?

Come to the table. Eat and drink. In the address of the body and blood to you, hear the shepherd's voice calling you by name, knowing you and your need. Here is the end of hunger and thirst, the beginning of the wiping away of all tears, the flowing of the spring of life-giving waters.

Gordon Lathrop

F OR the marriage of the Lamb has come,
and his Bride has made herself ready.   Revelation 19:7

B Y the cross death was slain and Adam was restored to
life. The cross is the glory of all the apostles, the crown
of the martyrs, the sanctification of the saints. By the cross
we put on Christ and cast aside our former self. By the cross
we, the sheep of Christ, have been gathered into one flock,   Theodore
destined for the sheepfolds of heaven.   Eighth century

J UST as I am, without one plea,
But that thy blood was shed for me,
And that thou bidd'st me come to thee,
O Lamb of God, I come, I come.

Just as I am, thou wilt receive,
Wilt welcome, pardon, cleanse, relieve;
Because thy promise I believe,   Charlotte Elliott
O Lamb of God, I come, I come.   Nineteenth century

L AMB of God, you take away the sins of the world:
have mercy on us.
Lamb of God, you take away the sins of the world: Ancient litany:
grant us peace.   Breaking of the Bread

H E is the Pascha of our salvation.
It is he who, in many, endured many things:
It is he that was in Abel murdered,
   and in Isaac bound,
   and in Jacob exiled,
   and in Joseph sold,
   and in Moses exposed,
   and in the lamb slain,
   and in David persecuted,
   and in the prophets dishonoured.
It is he that was enfleshed in a virgin,
   that was hanged on a tree,
   that was buried in the earth,
   that was raised from the dead,
   that was taken up to the heights of the heavens.
He is the lamb being slain;
he is the lamb that is speechless;
he is the one born from Mary the lovely ewe-lamb;
he is the one taken *from the flock*,
   and dragged *to slaughter*,
   and sacrificed *at evening*,
   and buried *at night*;
   who on the tree was *not broken*,
   in the earth was not dissolved,
   who arose from the dead,
   and raised up humankind from the grave below.

Melito of Sardis
Second century

FIFTH WEEK OF EASTER

DAY 29

Y OU shall be like a watered garden.

B UT Mary stayed outside the tomb weeping. And as she wept, she bent over into the tomb and saw two angels in white sitting there, one at the head and one at the feet where the body of Jesus had been. And they said to her, "Woman, why are you weeping?" She said to them, "They have taken my Lord, and I don't know where they laid him." When she had said this, she turned around and saw Jesus there, but did not know it was Jesus. Jesus said to her, "Woman, why are you weeping? Whom are you looking for?" She thought it was the gardener and said to him, "Sir, if you carried him away, tell me where you laid him, and I will take him." Jesus said to her, "Mary!" she turned and said to him in Hebrew, "Rabbouni," which means Teacher.

John 20:11–16

91

A FTER the anointing, then, it remains to go into the bath of sacred waters. After stripping you of your robe, the priest himself leads you down into the flowing waters. But why naked? He reminds you of your former nakedness, when you were in Paradise and you were not ashamed. For Holy Writ says: "Adam and Eve were naked and were not ashamed," until they took up the garment of sin, a garment heavy with abundant shame.

John Chrysostom
Fourth century

F AR to the East there is the sacred grove of paradise. It is always flooded with spring's soft sunshine. The weather continually remains most agreeable. Neither sorrow nor sickness nor death are known there.

The grove is watered by a crystal-clear spring; its high trees are laden with luscious fruit which never falls to the ground. A phoenix, the bird of paradise, is the grove's sole inhabitant.

At the first gleam of dawn this bird bathes in the limpid stream and drinks from the spring. Then it flies to the tree of life and there awaits the sunrise. It greets the first beam of sunlight with a song more beautiful than any earthly music. After the sun is fully risen, it beats its wings with a ringing sound as its wings glitter in the sunlight like a rainbow.

When a thousand years have passed, the phoenix senses that its course is run. It leaves its home and paradise, and flies into the world where death holds sway. Soon its wings have carried it to Phoenicia, where it stops to rest in some remote place. It selects the highest palm tree and builds there a nest to serve as a grave. Now the phoenix dies only in order that it might live, and be created anew. Therefore it gathers the finest spices of every land, beds itself therein, and dies. The carcass, being set on fire by the sun's heat, generates life as it burns to ashes. For in these ashes is the germ of new life. Soon there comes forth a milk-white egg which, transform-ing itself like the caterpillar into a butterfly, becomes a phoenix and nourishes itself on heavenly dew.

Whoever sees it is amazed by its beauty. Its plumage shimmers with beautiful colors, its eyes sparkle like a hyacinth, and a crown of light encircles its head. No bird, and certainly no animal, rivals it in glory. It is royal in appearance and though gigantic in size flies gracefully and without effort. Thus the phoenix appears to admiring eyes. The birds of the sky gather as an escort. But the phoenix flies back alone to its haven, the sacred grove of paradise.

The legend of the phoenix according to Lactantius

T HE Lord into his garden's come,
The spices yield a rich perfume,
The lilies grow and thrive.
Refreshing show'rs of grace divine
From Jesus flow to every vine,
And make the dead revive.

'Tis there we'll reign, and shout, and sing,
And make the upper regions ring
When all the saints get home;
Come on, come on, my brethren dear,
Soon we shall meet together there
For Jesus bids us come.

American folk hymn
Eighteenth century

DAY 30

Y OU are an enclosed garden.

W E are a Garden wall'd around,
Chosen and made peculiar Ground;
A little Spot inclos'd by Grace
Out of the World's wide Wilderness

Like Trees of Myrrh and Spice we stand,
Planted by God the Father's Hand;
And all his Springs in Sion flow,
To make the young Plantation grow.

Let my Beloved come, and taste
His pleasant Fruits at his own Feast.
I come, my Spouse, I come, he cries,
With Love and Pleasure in his Eyes.

Our Lord into his Garden comes,
Well pleas'd to smell our poor Perfumes,
And calls us to a Feast divine,
Sweeter than Honey, Milk, or Wine.

Eat of the Tree of Life, my Friends,
The Blessings that my Father sends;
Your Taste shall all my Dainties prove
And drink abundance of my Love.

Jesus, we will frequent thy Board,
And sing the Bounties of our Lord:
But the rich Food on which we live
Demands more Praise than Tongues can give.

Isaac Watts
Eighteenth century

A ND you, Jesus, good Lord, are you not also Mother? Would a mother not be one who, like a hen, gathers her young beneath her wings? In truth, Lord, you are my Mother!

Anselm of Canterbury
Eleventh century

A BOUT half an hour later—or it might have been half a hundred years later, for time there is not like time here—Lucy stood with her dear friend, her oldest Narnian friend, the Faun Tumnus, looking down over the wall of that garden, and seeing all Narnia spread out below. But when you looked down you found that this hill was much higher than you had thought: it sank down with shining cliffs, thousands of feet below them and trees in that lower world looked no bigger than grains of green salt. Then she turned inward again and stood with her back to the wall and looked at the garden.

"I see," she said at last, thoughtfully. "I see now. This garden is like the Stable. It is far bigger inside than it was outside."

"Of course, Daughter of Eve," said the Faun. The further up and the further in you go, the bigger everything gets. The inside is larger than the outside."

Lucy looked hard at the garden and saw that it was not really a garden at all but a whole world, with its own rivers and woods and sea and mountains. But they were not strange: she knew them all.

"I see," she said. "This is still Narnia, and, more real and more beautiful than the Narnia down below, just as *it* was more real and more beautiful than the Narnia outside the Stable door! I see . . . world within world, Narnia within Narnia. . . ."

"Yes," said Mr. Tumnus, "like an onion: except that as you continue to go in and in, each circle is larger than the last."

C. S. Lewis

ONE of the seven angels came and said to me, "Come here. I will show you the bride, the wife of the Lamb." He took me in spirit to a great, high mountain and showed me the holy city Jerusalem coming down out of heaven from God. It gleamed with the splendor of God. Its radiance was like that of a precious stone, like jasper, clear as crystal. It had a massive, high wall, with twelve gates where twelve angels were stationed and on which names were inscribed, the names of the twelve tribes of the Israelites. There were three gates facing east, three north, three south, and three west. The wall of the city had twelve courses of stones as its foundation, on which were inscribed the twelve names of the twelve apostles of the Lamb.

Revelation 21:9–14

GOD to enfold me,
God to surround me,
God in my speaking,
God in my thinking,
God in my sleeping,
God in my waking,
God in my watching,
God in my hoping,
God in my life,
God in my lips,
God in my soul,
God in my heart.

Celtic prayer

T O the victor I will give the right to eat from the tree of life
that is in the garden of God.

I am yearning for the time
When my right is all revealed—
Jesus Christ, true tree of life,
Fount of all our justice he;
My strong support, my second made,
No empty hope of fig-leaves' shade.

Ann Griffiths
Eighteenth century

R EMAIN in me, as I remain in you. Just as a branch cannot
bear fruit on its own unless it remains on the vine, so
neither can you unless you remain in me. I am the vine, you
are the branches.

John 15:4–5

A ND you, high eternal Trinity,
acted as if you were drunk with love,
infatuated with your creature.
When you saw that this tree could bear no fruit
but the fruit of death
because it was cut off from you who are life,
you came to its rescue
with the same love
with which you had created it:
you engrafted your divinity
into the dead tree of our humanity.
O sweet tender engrafting!
You, sweetness itself,
stooped to join yourself
with our bitterness.

Catherine of Siena
Fourteenth century

THOSE who gain the victory,
   I will feed from the tree of life
Liturgy of the Hours which grows in the garden of God.

THERE in God's garden stands the Tree of Wisdom,
   whose leaves hold forth the healing of the nations:
Tree of all knowledge,
   Tree of all compassion,
Tree of all beauty.

Its name is Jesus, name that says, "Our Saviour!"
There on its branches see the scars of suffering;
see where the tendrils
   of our human selfhood
feed on its lifeblood.

Thorns not his own are tangled in its foliage;
our greed has starved it, our despite has choked it.
Yet, look! It lives!
   Its grief has not destroyed it
nor fire consumed it.

See how its branches reach to us in welcome;
hear what the voice says, "Come to me, ye weary!
Give me your sickness;
   give me all your sorrow;
I will give blessing."

This is my ending, this my resurrection;
into your hands, Lord, I commit my spirit.
This have I searched for;
   now I can possess it.
Hungarian hymn This ground is holy.

B LESSED are they who wash their robes so as to have the right to the tree of life and enter the city through its gates.

Revelation 22:14

B Y thy cross, thou didst destroy the curse of the tree.
By thy burial thou didst slay the dominion of death.
By thy rising, thou didst enlighten the human race.
O benefactor, Christ our God, glory to thee.

Paschal vespers
Orthodox liturgy

DAY 32

H OW beautiful you are, how pleasing,
my love, my delight!

O eternal Father! O fiery abyss of charity! O eternal beauty, O eternal wisdom, O eternal goodness, O eternal mercy! O hope and refuge of sinners! O immeasurable generosity! O eternal, infinite Good! O mad lover! And you have need of your creature? It seems so to me, for you act as if you could not live without her, in spite of the fact that you are Life itself, and everything has life from you and nothing can have life without you. Why then are you so mad? Because you have fallen in love with what you have made! You are pleased and delighted over her within yourself, as if you were drunk with desire for her salvation. She runs away from you and you go looking for her. She strays and you draw closer to her. You clothed yourself in our humanity, and nearer than that you could not have come.

And what shall I say? I will stutter, "Ah—ah," because there is nothing else I know how to say.

Catherine of Siena
Fourteenth century

BATTER my heart, three-personed God; for You
As yet but knock, breathe, shine, and seek to mend;
That I may rise and stand, o'erthrow me, and bend
Your force, to break, blow, burn, and make me new.
I, like an usurped town, to another due,
Labor to admit You, but Oh, to no end!
Reason, Your viceroy in me, me should defend,
But is captived, and proves weak or untrue.
Yet dearly I love You, and would be loved fain,
But am betrothed unto Your enemy:
Divorce me, untie or break that knot again,
Take me to You, imprison me, for I,
Except You enthrall me, never shall be free,
Nor ever chaste, except You ravish me.

John Donne
Seventeenth century

WHILE it is alive
Until Death touches it
While it and I lap one Air
Dwell in one blood
Under one Sacrament
Show me Division can split or pare—

Love is like Life—merely longer
Love is like Death, during the Grave
Love is the Fellow of the Resurrection
Scooping up the Dust and chanting "Live!"

Emily Dickinson
Nineteenth century

AS soon as they come forth from those sacred waters, all
who are present embrace them, greet them, kiss them,
rejoice with them, and congratulate them, because those
who were heretofore slaves and captives have suddenly
become free people and children and have been invited to

the royal table. For straightway after they come up from the waters, they are led to the awesome table heavy laden with countless favors, where they taste of the Master's body and blood, and become a dwelling place for the Holy Spirit. Since they have put on Christ himself, wherever they go they are like angels on earth, rivalling the brilliance of the rays of the sun.

John Chrysostom
Fourth century

A CCORDING to a custom that is as old as the human race, a sign carried on the forehead is a sign of belonging. Slaves, especially, often had such a sign branded on their foreheads (or arms); it told others who their owner was. In the sacrament of baptism Jesus who suffered and died and conquered on the cross takes possession of the children whom their parents have brought to him. The children will belong to him not as slaves used to belong to their masters, but they will belong to Christ the way lovers belong to each other.

Balthasar Fischer

F OR Wisdom is mobile beyond all motion,
   and she penetrates and pervades all things by reason
      of her purity.
For she is an aura of the might of God
   and a pure effusion of the glory of the Almighty;
      therefore nought that is sullied enters into her.
For she is the refulgence of eternal light,
   the spotless mirror of the power of God,
   the image of his goodness.
And she, who is one, can do all things,
   and renews everything while herself perduring;
And passing into holy souls from age to age,
   she produces friends of God and prophets.
For there is nought God loves, be it not one who dwells

with Wisdom.
For she is fairer than the sun
    and surpasses every constellation of the stars.
Compared to light, she takes precedence;
    for that, indeed, night supplants,
    but wickedness prevails not over Wisdom.

Indeed, she reaches from end to end mightily
    and governs all things well.
Her I loved and sought after from my youth;
    I sought to take her for my bride
    and was enamored of her beauty.
She adds to nobility the splendor of companionship with
        God;

Wisdom 7:24—8:3   even the LORD of all loved her.

DAY 33

Y OU will live in my love.

A ND SO, now I call upon you, since I love you more,
  O Neophyte, dear to me, always be what you have
        been called, one newly baptized everywhere,
Pleasing on every occasion, beautiful always,
    Not a bridegroom today and unwed tomorrow,
Romanos   For this has married you to the Lord,
Sixth century   Our resurrection.

I N her greatest strength she is overcome; in her blindness, she sees most clearly; in her greatest clearness, she is both dead and alive. The richer she becomes, the poorer she is. . . . The more she storms, the more loving God is to her. The higher she soars, the more brightly she shines from the reflection of the Godhead. The more she labours, the more sweetly she rests. The more she understands, the less she speaks. The louder she calls, the greater wonders she works with his power and her might. The more God loves her, the more glorious the course of love, the nearer the resting place, the closer the embrace. The closer the embrace, the sweeter the kiss. The more lovingly they gaze at each other, the more difficult it is to part. The more he gives her, the more she spends, the more she has. The more humbly she takes leave, the sooner she returns. The more the fire burns, the more her light increases. The more love consumes her, the brighter she shines. The vaster God's praise, the vaster her desire for him.

Mechthild of
Magdeburg
Thirteenth century

W E the bridesmaids
  sing your praises,
happy woman, bride of God,
virgin still, Ecclesia.
Snow your body is, dark the waves of your hair,
sound, unblemished, lovely creature.

My purity intact for you, my lamp alight in my hand,
Bridegroom, I come out to meet you.

Decay is destroyed; disease,
with its pain and its tears, has gone.

Death is no more, folly has fled
and grief, that gnaws the mind,
is dead. A sudden shaft of joy
from Christ our God,
and now this mortal world is shining.

Methodius of Olympus
Third century

W HEN love is found
    and hope comes home,
sing and be glad
    that two are one.
When love explodes
    and fills the sky,
praise God and share
    our Maker's joy.

When love has flowered
    in trust and care,
build both each day
    that love may dare
to reach beyond
    home's warmth and light,
to serve and strive
    for truth and right.

When love is tried
    as loved-ones change,
hold still to hope
    though all seems strange,
till ease returns
    and love grows wise
through listening ears
    and opened eyes.

When love is torn
    and trust betrayed,
pray strength to love
    till torments fade,
till lovers keep
    no score of wrong
but hear through pain
    love's Easter song.

Praise God for love,
   praise God for life,
in age or youth,
   in husband, wife.
Lift up your hearts.
   Let love be fed
through death and life
   in broken bread.   Brian Wren

W HEN the girl's parents left the bedroom and closed the
    door behind them, Tobiah arose from bed and said to
his wife, "My love, get up. Let us pray and beg our Lord to
have mercy on us and to grant us deliverance." She got up,
and they started to pray and beg that deliverance might be
theirs. He began with these words:

"Blessed are you, O God of our fathers;
praised be your name forever and ever.
Let the heavens and all your creation
   praise you forever.
You made Adam and you gave him his wife Eve
   to be his help and support;
   and from these two the human race descended.
You said, 'It is not good for the man to be alone;
   let us make him a partner like himself.'
Now, Lord, you know that I take this wife of mine
   not because of lust,
   but for a noble purpose.
Call down your mercy on me and on her,
   and allow us to live together to a happy old age."

They said together, "Amen, amen," and went to bed for the
night.   Tobit 8:4–9

DAY 34

R EFRESH me with apples,
   for I am faint with love.

B UT now Christ has been raised from the dead, the
   firstfruits of those who have fallen asleep. For since
death came through a human being, the resurrection of the
dead came also through a human being. For just as in Adam
all die, so too in Christ shall all be brought to life, but each
one in proper order: Christ the firstfruits; then, at his coming,
those who belong to Christ; then comes the end, when he
hands over the kingdom to his God and Father, when he has
destroyed every sovereignty and every authority and power.

1 Corinthians
15:20–24

I speak to you who have just been reborn in baptism, my
  little children in Christ, you who are the new offspring of
the church, gift of the Father, proof of Mother Church's
fruitfulness. All of you who stand fast in the Lord are a holy
seed, a new colony of bees, the very flower of our ministry
and fruit of our toil, my joy and my crown.

Augustine
Fourth century

P ICTURE in your mind a tree whose roots are watered by
   an ever-flowing fountain that becomes a great and living
river with four channels to water the garden of the entire
church. From the trunk of this tree, imagine that there are
growing twelve branches that are adorned with leaves,
flowers and fruit. This is the fruit that took its origin from the
Virgin's womb and reached its savory maturity on the tree of
the cross under the midday heat of the Eternal Sun, that is,
the love of Christ. In the garden of the heavenly paradise—
God's table—this fruit is served to those who desire it.

Bonaventure
Thirteenth century

PLANTATION of God,
holy vineyard of his catholic church,

you the chosen who have put your confidence
in the simplicity of the fear of the Lord,

you who have become, through faith,
heirs of his everlasting kingdom,

you who have received the power and gift of his Spirit,
who have been armed by him,
who have been strengthened in fear,

you who share in the pure and precious blood
poured out by the great God, Jesus Christ,

you who have received the freedom
to call the almighty God "Father,"
who are coheirs and friends of his beloved Son:

listen to the teaching of God,
all you who hope in his promises
and wait for their fulfillment!

Didascalia of the
Apostles
Third century

THE church rejoices in the redemption of many, and is
glad with spiritual exultation that the members of her
household are at hand dressed in white. You have this in the
Canticle of Canticles. Rejoicing, she invokes Christ, having
prepared a banquet, which seems worthy of heavenly feasting. And so she says: "Let my beloved come into his garden
and eat the fruits of his apple trees." What are these apple
trees? You were made dry wood in Adam, but now through
the grace of Christ you flower as apple trees.

Ambrose
Fourth century

THE tree of life my soul hath seen,
Laden with fruit, and always green:
The trees of nature fruitless be
Compared with Christ the apple tree.

His beauty doth all things excel:
By faith I know, but ne'er can tell,
The glory which I now can see
In Jesus Christ the apple tree.

For happiness I long have sought,
And pleasure dearly I have bought:
I missed of all; but now I see
'Tis found in Christ the apple tree.

I'm weary with my former toil,
Here I will sit and rest a while:
Under the shadow I will be,
Of Jesus Christ the apple tree.

This fruit doth make my soul to thrive,
It keeps my dying faith alive;
Which makes my soul in haste to be
With Jesus Christ the apple tree.

American folk hymn
Eighteenth century

COME, my lover, let us go forth to the fields
and spend the night among the villages.
Let us go early to the vineyards,
    and see if the vines are in bloom,
If the buds have opened,
    if the pomegranates have blossomed;
There will I give you my love.
The mandrakes give forth fragrance,
    and at our doors are all choice fruits;
Both fresh and mellowed fruits, my lover,
Song of Songs 7:11–14   I have kept in store for you.

Y OU are a garden fountain, a well of water flowing fresh
from Lebanon.

B EHOLD, God is my salvation;
I will trust, and will not be afraid;
for the LORD God is my strength and my song,
and has become my salvation.
With joy you will draw water from the wells of
salvation.   Isaiah 12:2

L OVE the dispossessed, all those who, living amid human
injustice, thirst after justice. Jesus had special concern
for them. Have no fear of being disturbed by them.   Rule of Taizé

S OME one was drawing water and my teacher placed my
hand under the spout. As the cool stream gushed over
one hand she spelled into the other the word *water*, first
slowly, then rapidly. I stood still, my whole attention fixed
upon the motions of her fingers. Suddenly I felt a misty
consciousness as of something forgotten—a thrill of returning thought; and somehow the mystery of language was
revealed to me. I knew that w-a-t-e-r meant the wonderful
cool something that was flowing over my hand. That living
word awakened my soul, gave it light, hope, joy, set it free.   Helen Keller

S O he came to a town of Samaria called Sychar, near the plot of land that Jacob had given to his son Joseph. Jacob's well was there. Jesus, tired from his journey, sat down there at the well. It was about noon.

A woman of Samaria came to draw water. Jesus said to her, "Give me a drink."

John 4:5–7

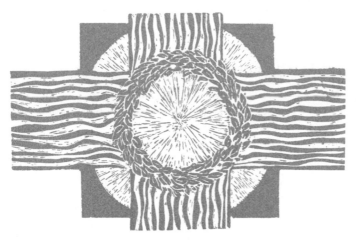

SIXTH
WEEK
OF
EASTER

DAY 36

B RING me, O king, to your chambers.

B UT one thing more I preach unto you. My throne before
which you shall presently stand after your baptism
before the Great Sanctuary is a foretype of the future glory.
The psalmody with which you will be received is a prelude
to the psalmody of heaven; the lamps which you will kindle
are a sacrament of the illumination there with which we
shall meet the Bridegroom, shining and virgin souls, with
the lamps of our faith shining, not sleeping through our
carelessness, that we may not miss him that we look for if he
comes unexpectedly; nor yet unfed, and without oil, and
destitute of good works, that we be not cast out of the bride-
chamber.

Gregory of Nazianzus
Fourth century

CROWN him with many crowns,
The Lamb upon his throne;
Hark, how the heav'nly anthem drowns
All music but its own.
Awake, my soul, and sing
Of him who died for thee,
And hail him as thy matchless king
Through all eternity.

Crown him the Lord of peace,
Whose pow'r a scepter sways
From pole to pole, that wars may cease,
Absorbed in prayer and praise.
His reign shall know no end,
And round his pierced feet
Fair flow'rs of paradise extend
Their fragrance ever sweet.

Crown him the Lord of years,
The potentate of time,
Creator of the rolling spheres,
Ineffably sublime.
All hail, Redeemer, hail!
For thou hast died for me;
Thy praise and glory shall not fail
Throughout eternity.

Matthew Bridges
Nineteenth century

WHAT if our God were Queen of heaven?

If our God were Queen of heaven, we could burn incense to
her and bake cakes for her, and our adoration would be
acceptable.

If our God were Queen of heaven, her crown would rest on
hair long and curly and rainbowed, and we could grab on to
that hair as we nursed and so be saved from falling. Her

shining face, smooth and clear as light, would enliven the universe. And when we were poor, the Queen would take from her necklace flowing with pearls and opals and every colored gem perhaps an amber to fill our needs. The resplendent gold of her majestic robe would be what we call the sun, and the sheen of her nightdress the moon. Her rule would reach to the deepest corners of the darkness; her beauty would rout the devils and her wisdom rear the world. Her royal blood would give us divinity. Our being born again in God would be a nativity from the divine womb, God's labor an agony of necessity; for we know it is the essence of the reign of our Queen to love with mercy. Our death would be, as with all babies, a going home to mother. Our life would be, as with heirs apparent, following in the train of the Queen.

The beauty of the Sovereign has terrified the world. She has borne us in pain and nursed us with care; and we, like Jewish children, carry her blood and are royal from rebirth in her. For our God is Queen of all the earth, and adoration of her splendor is our life.

Gail Ramshaw

U NTO Me?" I do not know you—
Where may be your House?

"I am Jesus—Late of Judea—
Now—of Paradise"—

Wagons—have you—to convey me?
This is far from Thence—

"Arms of Mine—sufficient Phaeton—
Trust Omnipotence"—

I am spotted—"I am Pardon"—
I am small—"The Least
Is esteemed in Heaven the Chiefest—
Occupy my House"—

Emily Dickinson
Nineteenth century

DAY 37

O N the throne sat one whose appearance sparkled like jasper and carnelian.

J ERUSALEM the golden, with milk and honey blest,
   beneath thy contemplation sink heart
      and voice oppressed:
I know not, oh, I know not, what joys await us there,
what radiancy of glory, what bliss beyond compare.

There is the throne of David; and there,
      from care released,
the shout of them that triumph,
      the song of them that feast;
and they who with their Leader have conquered
      in the fight,
for ever and for ever are clad in robes of white.

Oh, sweet and blessed country,
      the home of God's elect!
Oh, sweet and blessed country that eager hearts expect!
Jesus, in mercy bring us to that dear land of rest,
who art, with God the Father, and Spirit, ever blest.

Bernard of Cluny
Twelfth century

H OLY Mary
   Holy Mother of God
Mirror of justice
Throne of wisdom
Mystical Rose
Tower of ivory
Ark of the covenant
Gate of heaven
Litany of Loreto   Morning star

H E is King of kings,
He is Lord of lords.
Jesus Christ, the first and last,
No one works like him.

He built his throne up in the air,
No one works like him.
And called his saints from everywhere,
No one works like him.

He pitched his tent on Canaan ground,
No one works like him.
And broke the Roman kingdom down,
No one works like him.

Afro-American
spiritual

N OW glad of heart be ev'ry one!
The fight is fought, the day is won,
The Christ is set upon the throne.

Who on the rood was crucified,
Who rose again, as at this tide,
In glory to the Father's side.

Who baffled death and harrowed hell
And led the souls that love him well
All in the light of lights to dwell.

To him we lift our heart and voice
And in his paradise rejoice
With harp and pipe and happy noise.

Then rise, all Christian folk, with me
And carol forth the One-in-Three
That was and is and is to be.

Easter carol
Fourteenth century

YOUR throne stands firm from of old;
from everlasting you are, O LORD.
The floods lift up, O LORD,
the floods lift up their voice;
the floods lift up their tumult.
More powerful than the roar of many waters,
more powerful than the breakers of the sea—
powerful on high is the LORD.
Your decrees are worthy of trust indeed:
holiness befits your house,
Psalm 93:2–5   O LORD, for length of days.

DAY 38

WISDOM has dressed her meat, mixed her wine, yes,
she has spread her table.

COME away to the skies, my beloved, arise
and rejoice in the day thou wast born;
on this festival day, come exulting away,
and with singing to Zion return.

For the glory we were first created to share,
both the nature and kingdom divine!
Now created again that our lives may remain,
throughout time and eternity thine.

We with thanks do approve the design of that love
which hath joined us to Jesus' name;
so united in heart, let us nevermore part,
American folk hymn   till we meet at the feast of the Lamb.

J OIN, then, all of you, join in our Master's rejoicing.
You who were the first to come, you who came after,
come and collect now your wages.
The rich and the poor, sing and dance together.
You that are hard on yourselves, you that are easy,
honour this day.
You that have fasted and you that have not,
make merry today.

The meal is ready: come and enjoy it.
The calf is a fat one: you will not go hungry away.
There's kindness for all to partake of and kindness
        to spare.

Away with pleading of poverty:
the kingdom belongs to us all.
Away with bewailing of failings:
forgiveness has come from the grave.
Away with your fears of dying:
the death of our Saviour has freed us from fear.
Death played the master: he has mastered death.

Anonymous paschal
homily
Fourth century

O NE of his fellow guests on hearing this said to him,
"Blessed is the one who will dine in the kingdom of
God." He replied to him, "A man gave a great dinner to
which he invited many. When the time for the dinner came,
he dispatched his servant to say to those invited, 'Come,
everything is now ready.' But one by one, they all began to
excuse themselves. The first said to him, 'I have purchased a
field and must go to examine it; I ask you, consider me
excused.' And another said, 'I have purchased five yoke of
oxen and am on my way to evaluate them; I ask you,
consider me excused.' And another said, 'I have just married
a woman, and therefore I cannot come.' The servant went
and reported this to his master. Then the master of the house
in a rage commanded his servant, 'Go out quickly into the

streets and alleys of the town and bring in here the poor and the crippled, the blind and the lame.' The servant reported, 'Sir, your orders have been carried out and still there is room.' The master then ordered the servant, 'Go out to the highways and hedgerows and make people come in that my home may be filled.'"

Luke 14:15–23

DAY 39

T HIS day I have begotten you.

B EHOLD, I will bring them from the north country,
and gather them from the farthest parts of the earth,
among them the blind and the lame,
    the woman with child and her who is in labor, together;
    a great company, they shall return here.
With weeping they shall come,
    and with consolations I will lead them back,
I will make them walk by brooks of water,
    in a straight path in which they shall not stumble:
for I am as a father to Israel,
    and Ephraim is as my first-born.

Hear the word of the LORD, O nations,
    and declare it in the coastlands afar off;
say, "The one who scattered Israel's people will
        gather them
    and will keep them as a shepherd keeps the flock."
For the LORD has ransomed Jacob,

and has redeemed Jacob from hands too strong
   for them.
They shall come and sing aloud on the height of Zion,
   and they shall be radiant over the goodness of the LORD,
over the grain, the wine, and the oil,
   and over the young of the flock and the herd;
their life shall be like a watered garden,
   and they shall languish no more.
Then shall the maidens rejoice in the dance,
   and the young men and the old shall be merry.
I will turn their mourning into joy,
   I will comfort them, and give them gladness for sorrow.   Jeremiah 31:8–13

So you shall say to Pharaoh: Thus says the LORD: Israel is
my son, my first-born. Hence I tell you: Let my son go,
that he may serve me.   Exodus 4:22–23

O Christ,
  you take upon yourself all our burdens
so that,
freed of all that weighs us down,
we can constantly begin anew to walk,
with lightened step,
from worry towards trusting,
from the shadows towards the clear flowing waters,
from our own will
towards the vision of the coming kingdom.
And then we know,
though we hardly dared hope so,
that you offer to make every human being
a reflection of your face.   Roger Schutz

F IRST, there is the church. First, there is the church. *First, there is the church.* This is not a typographical error. It has to be repeated (more times than above) because of a more fundamental error in our past and in our present. Christians simply cannot think straight or act right about any type of ministry *within the church,* unless we first get some very wrong notions out of our heads and hearts and bones and marrow.

Somewhere along the line, we fell into an unbiblical and unChristian trap. And we got the idea that ministers come first . . . and only then the church. We got the crazy idea that God makes bishops (including the pope) first, and then bishops and priests somehow create the church, the community of believers. We never put it that crudely. But that is about the way many of us think . . . and act.

Now we have to clear the air and begin to understand and feel again what was understood and felt for so long: that God covenants a people, a church, a community of initiated (baptized, confirmed, eucharistized) people. That is the grand and beautiful reality of grace and mission and sign—a people created in covenant worship to witness and to serve. That is what we have to get into our heads and bones and feelings again. Until we do, nothing we say about any ministry will make Christian sense.

Robert W. Hovda

A LL of us must examine our way of living in light of the needs of the poor. Christian faith and the norms of justice impose distinct limits on what we consume and how we view material goods. The great wealth of the United States can easily blind us to the poverty that exists in this nation and the destitution of hundreds of millions of people in other parts of the world. Americans are challenged today as never before to develop the inner freedom to resist the temptation constantly to seek more. Only in this way will the nation avoid what Paul VI called "the most evident form of moral underdevelopment," namely, greed.

Economic Justice
for All

F OR those who are led by the Spirit of God are children of God. For you did not receive a spirit of slavery to fall back into fear, but you received a spirit of adoption, through which we cry, *Abba*, "Father!" The Spirit itself bears witness with our spirit that we are children of God, and if children, then heirs, heirs of God and joint heirs with Christ, if only we suffer with him so that we may also be glorified with him.   Romans 8:14–17

S OAR we now where Christ has led,
Following our exalted Head;
Made like him, like him we rise;
Ours the cross, the grave, the skies!

Charles Wesley
Eighteenth century

DAY 40

I will give you the crown of life.

W HEN they had come together, they asked Jesus, "Lord, will you at this time restore dominion to Israel?" Jesus said to them, "It is not for you to know times or seasons which the Father has fixed by divine authority. But you shall receive power when the Holy Spirit has come upon you; and you shall be my witnesses in Jerusalem and in all Judea and Samaria and to the end of the earth." And when he had said this, as they were looking on, Jesus was lifted up, and a cloud took him out of their sight. And while they were gazing into heaven as he went, behold, two men stood by them in white robes, and said, "O Galileans, why do you stand looking into heaven? This Jesus, who was taken up from you into heaven, will come in the same way as you saw him go into heaven."   Acts 1:6–11

A LL you peoples clap your hands,
shout to God with cries of gladness.
God mounts [the] throne amid shouts of joy;
the LORD, amid trumpet blasts.
Sing praise to God, sing praise;

Psalm 47:2, 6–7   sing praise to our king, sing praise.

Q UEEN of heaven, rejoice, alleluia.
For Christ, your Son and Son of God,
has risen as he said, alleluia.
Pray to God for us, alleluia.

Regina Caeli   Rejoice and be glad, O Virgin Mary, alleluia.
Twelfth century   For the Lord has truly risen, alleluia.

B ECAUSE I have heard of your faith in the Lord Jesus and
your love toward all the saints, I do not cease to give
thanks for you, remembering you in my prayers, that the
God of our Lord Jesus Christ, the Father of glory, may give
you a spirit of wisdom and of revelation, that you may know
God, having the eyes of your hearts enlightened, that you
may know what is the hope to which God has called you,
what are the riches of God's glorious inheritance in the
saints, and what is the immeasurable greatness of God's
power in us who believe, according to the working of God's
great might which was accomplished in Christ when God
raised Christ from the dead and made him sit at the right
hand of power in the heavenly places, far above all rule and
authority and power and dominion, and above every name
that is named, not only in this age but also in that which is to
come; and God has put all things under the feet of Christ and
has made him the head over all things for the church, which
Ephesians 1:15–23   is the body of Christ, the fullness of the one who fills all in all.

W E sing of God, the mighty source
of all things; the stupendous force
on which all strength depends;
from whose right arm, beneath whose eyes,
all period, power, and enterprise
commences, reigns, and ends.

Glorious the sun in mid career;
glorious the assembled fires appear;
glorious the comet's train:
glorious the trumpet and alarm;
glorious the almighty stretch-out arm;
glorious the enraptured main:

Glorious, most glorious, is the crown
of him that brought salvation down
by meekness, Mary's son;
seers that stupendous truth believed,
and now the matchless deed's achieved,   Christopher Smart
determined, dared, and done.   Eighteenth century

A NOTHER distinctive custom, this one in the East, was the
practice of placing garlands of flowers on the heads of
the newly baptised. Probably borrowed from secular life, it
was widespread already in the fourth century, so its origin
was probably much earlier. In secular life, garlanding was a
sign of victory, triumph and joy (e.g., winning sports events
in the arena, etc.). The same idea was transferred to the
spiritual realm where the garland signified the heavenly
crown of glory and incorruptibility, the crown of invincible
faith, of strength and of justice, imparted through baptism.   Casimir Kucharek

Y OU shall be called by a new name
pronounced by the mouth of the LORD.
You shall be a glorious crown in the hand of the LORD,

Isaiah 62:2–3   a royal diadem held by your God.

DAY 41

A shield before me is God.

I renounce thee, Satan." What has happened? What is this
strange and unexpected turn of events? Although you
were all quivering with fear, did you rebel against your
master? Did you look with scorn upon his cruelty? Who has
brought you to such madness? Whence came this boldness
of yours? "I have a weapon," you say, "a strong weapon."
What weapon, what ally? Tell me! "I enter into thy service, O
Christ," you reply. "Hence, I am bold and rebel. For I have a
strong place of refuge. This has made me superior to the

John Chrysostom   demon, although heretofore I was trembling and afraid.
Fourth century   Therefore, I not only renounce him but also all his pomps."

P UT on the armor of God so that you may be able to stand
firm against the tactics of the devil. For our struggle is not
with flesh and blood but with the principalities, with the
powers, with the world rulers of this present darkness, with
the evil spirits in the heavens. Therefore, put on the armor of
God, that you may be able to resist on the evil day and,
having done everything, to hold your ground. So stand fast
with your loins girded in truth, clothed with righteousness as
a breastplate, and your feet shod in readiness for the gospel

of peace. In all circumstances, hold faith as a shield, to quench all the flaming arrows of the evil one. And take the helmet of salvation and the sword of the Spirit, which is the word of God.

With all prayer and supplication, pray at every opportunity in the Spirit.   Ephesians 6:11–18

L ET us, therefore, take courage and strip ourselves for the contests. Christ has put on us armor that is more glittering than any gold, stronger than any steel, hotter and more violent than any fire, and lighter than any breath of air. The nature of this armor does not burden and bend our knees, but it gives wings to our limbs and lifts them up. If you wish to take flight to heaven, this armor is no hindrance. It is a new kind of armor, since it is a new kind of combat.

Although I am human, I must aim my blows at demons; although clad in flesh, my struggle is with incorporeal powers. On this account God has made my breastplate not from metal but from justice; God has prepared for me a shield which is made not of bronze but of faith. I have, too, a sharp sword, the word of the Spirit.   John Chrysostom
                                                              Fourth century

Q UICKLY the knight rose. He drew his sharp sword and struck the dragon's head so fiercely that it seemed nothing could withstand the blow. The dragon's crest was too hard to take a cut, but he wanted no more such blows. He tried to fly away and could not because of his wounded wing.

Loudly he bellowed—the like was never heard before— and from his body, like a wide devouring oven, sent a flame of fire that scorched the knight's face and heated his armor red-hot. Faint, weary, sore, burning with heat and wounds, the knight fell to the ground, ready to die, and the dragon clapped his iron wings in victory, while the lady, watching from afar, fell to her knees. She thought that her champion had lost the battle.

But it happened that where the knight fell, an ancient spring of silvery water bubbled from the ground. In that cool water the knight lay resting until the sun rose. Then he, too, rose to do battle again. And when the dragon saw him, he could hardly believe his eyes. Could this be the same knight, he wondered, or another who had come to take his place?

The legend of Saint George and the dragon

D ONE is the battle on the dragon's back;
Our champion Christ confounded hath his foes.
The gates of hell are opened with a crack;
The sign triumphal raised is of the cross.
The devils tremble with hideous voice;
The souls are ransomed and to bliss can go.
Christ with his blood our ransom doth endorse:
Surrexit Dominus de sepulchro!

*William Dunbar
Sixteenth century*

G UIDE me ever, great Redeemer,
Pilgrim through this barren land.
I am weak, but you are mighty;
Hold me with your pow'rful hand.
Bread of heaven, bread of heaven,
Feed me now and evermore,
    Feed me now and evermore.

Open now the crystal fountain
Where the healing waters flow;
Let the fire and cloudy pillar
Lead me all my journey through.
Strong deliv'rer, strong deliv'rer,

Shield me with your mighty arm,
　Shield me with your mighty arm.

When I tread the verge of Jordan,
Bid my anxious fears subside;
Death of death and hell's destruction,
Land me safe on Canaan's side.
Songs and praises, songs and praises,
I will raise forevermore,
　　I will raise forevermore.

William Williams
Eighteenth century

DAY 42

T HE angel then showed me the river of life-giving water, clear as crystal, which issued from the throne of God.

A WE-INSPIRING, in truth, are the mysteries of the church; awesome, in truth, her altar. A fountain sprang up out of paradise, sending forth sensible streams; a fountain arises from this table, sending forth spiritual streams. Beside this fountain there have grown, not willows without fruit, but trees reaching to heaven itself, with fruit ever in season and incorrupt. If someone is intensely hot, let him come to this fountain and cool down the feverish heat. It dispels parching heat and gently cools all things that are very hot; not those inflamed by the sun's heat, but those set on fire by burning arrows. It does so because it takes its beginning from above, and has its source from there, and from there it is fed. Many are the streams of this fountain, streams which the Paraclete sends forth; and the Son becomes its Custodian.

John Chrysostom
Fourth century

How well I know that flowing spring in black of night.

The eternal fountain is unseen.
How well I know where she has been in black of night.

I do not know her origin.
None. Yet in her all things begin in black of night.

I know that nothing is so fair
and earth and firmament drink there in black of night.

I know that none can wade inside
to find her bright bottomless tide in black of night.

Her shining never has a blur;
I know that all light comes from her in black of night.

I know her streams converge and swell
and nourish people, skies and hell in black of night.

The stream whose birth is in this source
I know has a gigantic force in black of night.

The stream from but these two proceeds
yet neither one, I know, precedes in black of night.

The eternal fountain is unseen
in living bread that gives us being in black of night.

She calls on humankind to start
to drink her water, though in dark, for black is night.

O living fountain that I crave,
in bread of life I see her flame in black of night.

John of the Cross
Sixteenth century

BEARING life and more fruitful than paradise,
brighter than any royal chamber;
thy tomb, O Christ, is the fountain of our resurrection.

Troparion
Orthodox liturgy

I 'VE just come from the fountain,
I've just come from the fountain,
I've just come from the fountain,
His name's so sweet!

Been drinking from the fountain,
Been drinking from the fountain,
Been drinking from the fountain,
His name's so sweet!

Afro-American
spiritual

T HEN John saw the river, and the multitude was there. And now they had undergone a change; their robes were ragged, and stained with the road they had traveled, and stained with unholy blood; the robes of some barely covered their nakedness; and some indeed were naked. And some stumbled on the smooth stones at the river's edge, for they were blind; and some crawled with a terrible wailing, for they were lame; some did not cease to pluck at their flesh, which was rotten with running sores. All struggled to get to the river, in a dreadful hardness of heart: the strong struck down the weak, the ragged spat on the naked, the naked cursed the blind, the blind crawled over the lame. And someone cried: *"Sinner, do you love my Lord?"*

Then John saw the Lord—for a moment only; and the darkness, for a moment only, was filled with a light he could not bear. Then, in a moment, he was set free; his tears sprang as from a fountain; his heart, like a fountain of waters, burst. Then he cried: "Oh, blessed Jesus! Oh, Lord Jesus! Take me through!"

Of tears there was, yes, a very fountain—springing from a depth never sounded before, from depths John had not known were in him. And he wanted to rise up, singing, singing in that great morning, the morning of his new life. Ah, how his tears ran down, how they blessed his soul!—as he felt himself, out of the darkness, and the fire, and the terrors of death, rising upward to meet the saints.

"Oh, yes!" cried the voice of Elisha. "Bless our God forever!"

And a sweetness filled John as he heard this voice, and heard the sound of singing: the singing was for him. For his drifting soul was anchored in the love of God; in the rock that endured forever. The light and the darkness had kissed each other, and were married now, forever, in the life and the vision of John's soul.

I, John, saw a city, way in the middle of the air,

James Baldwin   *Waiting, waiting, waiting up there.*

F OR it is not only Peter but the whole Church that binds and looses from sin; and as for the sublime teaching of John about the Word, who in the beginning was God with God, and everything else he told us about Christ's divinity, and about the trinity and unity of the Godhead, which now, until the Lord comes, is all like a faint reflection in a mirror, but which will be seen face to face in the kingdom of heaven—it was not only John who drank in this teaching that came forth from the Lord's breast as from a fountain. All who belong to the Lord are to drink it in.

Augustine
Fourth century

SEVENTH WEEK OF EASTER

W E are the temple of the living God.

S OLOMON stood before the altar of the LORD in the presence of the whole community of Israel, and stretching forth his hands toward heaven, he said, "If the heavens and the highest heavens cannot contain you, how much less this temple which I have built! Look kindly on the prayer and petition of your servant, O LORD, my God, and listen to the cry of supplication which I, your servant, utter before you this day. May your eyes watch night and day over this temple, the place where you have decreed you shall be honored; may you heed the prayer which I, your servant, offer in this place. Listen to the petitions of your servant and of your people Israel which they offer in this place. Listen from your heavenly dwelling and grant pardon."

1 Kings 8:22, 27–30

O Holy Ghost, whose temple I
Am, but of mud walls, and condensed dust,
And being sacrilegiously
Half wasted with youth's fires, of pride and lust,
    Must with new storms be weather-beat;
    Double in my heart thy flame,
Which let devout sad tears intend; and let
(Though this glass lanthorn, flesh, do suffer maim)
Fire, Sacrifice, Priest, Altar be the same.

John Donne
Seventeenth century

A LL Solomon's sea of brass and world of stone
Is not so dear to thee as one good groan.

George Herbert
Seventeenth century

S O then you are no longer strangers and sojourners, but
you are fellow citizens with the holy ones and members
of the household of God, built upon the foundation of the
apostles and prophets, with Christ Jesus himself as the
capstone. Through him the whole structure is held together
and grows into a temple sacred in the Lord; in him you also
are being built together into a dwelling place of God in the
Spirit.

Ephesians 2:19–22

Y OU have approached Mount Zion and the city of the
living God, the heavenly Jerusalem, and countless
angels in festal gathering, and the assembly of the firstborn
enrolled in heaven, and God the judge of all, and the spirits
of the just made perfect, and Jesus, the mediator of a new
covenant, and the sprinkled blood that speaks more elo-
quently than that of Abel.

Hebrews 12:22–24

W HEN they entered [Jerusalem] they went to the upper room where they were staying, Peter and John and James and Andrew, Philip and Thomas, Bartholomew and Matthew, James son of Alphaeus, Simon the Zealot, and Judas son of James. All these devoted themselves with one accord to prayer, together with some women, and Mary the mother of Jesus, and his brothers.   Acts 1:13–14

M AY is Mary's month, and I
  Muse at that and wonder why:
   Her feasts follow reason,
   Dated due to season—

Candlemas, Lady Day;
But the Lady Month, May,
   Why fasten that upon her,
   With a feasting in her honour?

Is it only its being brighter
Than the most are must delight her?
   Is it opportunest
   And flowers finds soonest?

Ask of her, the mighty mother:
Her reply puts this other
   Question: What is Spring?
   Growth in every thing—

Flesh and fleece, fur and feather,
Grass and greenworld all together;
   Star-eyed strawberry-breasted
   Throstle above her nested

Cluster of bugle blue eggs thin
Forms and warms the life within;

And bird and blossom swell
In sod or sheath or shell.

All things rising, all things sizing
Mary sees, sympathising
With that world of good,
Nature's motherhood.

Their magnifying of each its kind
With delight calls to mind
How she did in her stored
Magnify the Lord.

Well but there was more than this:
Spring's universal bliss
Much, had much to say
To offering Mary May.

When drop-of-blood-and-foam-dapple
Bloom lights the orchard-apple
And thicket and thorp are merry
With silver-surféd cherry.

And azuring-over greybell makes
Wood banks and brakes wash wet like lakes
And magic cuckoocall
Caps, clears, and clinches all—

This ecstasy all through mothering earth
Tells Mary her mirth till Christ's birth
To remember and exultation
In God who was her salvation.

Gerard Manley
Hopkins
Nineteenth century

MAY we be filled with the good things of your house, the holy things of your temple!

WHEN everyone has answered "Amen," the deacon says: "Attend!" The bishop then addresses the people with these words: "Holy things to the holy!" The people answer:
    One only Holy One, one only Lord,
    Jesus Christ, who is blessed for ever,
    to the glory of the Father. Amen.

The Apostolic
Constitutions
Fourth century

THE higher Christian churches—where, if anywhere, I belong—come at God with an unwarranted air of professionalism, with authority and pomp, as though they knew what they were doing, as though people in themselves were an appropriate set of creatures to have dealings with God. I often think of the set pieces of liturgy as certain words which people have successfully addressed to God without their getting killed. In the high churches they saunter through the liturgy like Mohawks along a strand of scaffolding who have long since forgotten their danger. If God were to blast such a service to bits, the congregation would be, I believe, genuinely shocked. But in the low churches you expect it any minute. This is the beginning of wisdom.

Annie Dillard

CHRISTIANS are indistinguishable from other people either by nationality, language or customs. They do not inhabit separate cities of their own, or speak a strange dialect, or follow some outlandish way of life. Their teaching is not based upon reveries inspired by curiosity. Unlike some other people, they champion no purely human doctrine. With regard to dress, food and manner of life in general, they follow the customs of whatever city they happen to be living in, whether it is Greek or foreign.

And yet there is something extraordinary about their lives. They live in their own countries as though they were only passing through. They play their full role as citizens, but labor under all the disabilities of aliens. Any country can be their homeland, but for them their homeland, wherever it may be, is a foreign country. Like others, they marry and have children, but they do not expose them. They share their meals, but not their wives. They live in the flesh, but they are not governed by the desires of the flesh. They pass their days upon earth, but they are citizens of heaven. Obedient to the laws, they yet live on a level that transcends the law.

Christians love all, but all persecute them. Condemned because they are not understood, they are put to death, but raised to life again. They live in poverty, but enrich many; they are totally destitute, but possess an abundance of everything. They suffer dishonor, but that is their glory. They are defamed, but vindicated. A blessing is their answer to abuse, deference their response to insult. For the good they do they receive the punishment of malefactors, but even then they rejoice, as though receiving the gift of life.

Letter to Diognetus
Second century

Day 45

I saw water flowing out from beneath the threshold of the temple.

Now since it was preparation day, in order that the bodies might not remain on the cross on the sabbath, for the sabbath day of that week was a solemn one, the Jews asked Pilate that their legs be broken and they be taken down. So the soldiers came and broke the legs of the first and then of the other one who was crucified with Jesus. But when they came to Jesus and saw that he was already dead, they did not break his legs, but one soldier thrust his lance into his side, and immediately blood and water flowed out.

John 19:31–34

O R are you unaware that we who were baptized into Christ Jesus were baptized into his death? We were indeed buried with him through baptism into death, so that, just as Christ was raised from the dead by the glory of the Father, we too might live in newness of life.

For if we have grown into union with him through a death like his, we shall also be united with him in the resurrection. We know that our old self was crucified with him, so that our sinful body might be done away with, that we might no longer be in slavery to sin. For a dead person has been absolved from sin. If, then, we have died with Christ, we believe that we shall also live with him. We know that Christ, raised from the dead, dies no more; death no longer has power over him. As to his death, he died to sin once and for all; as to his life, he lives for God. Consequently, you too must think of yourselves as being dead to sin and living for God in Christ Jesus.

Romans 6:3–11

W HENEVER water appears [in dreams or visions] it is usually the water of life, meaning a medium through which one is reborn. It symbolizes a sort of baptism cere-mony, or initiation, a healing bath that gives resurrection or rebirth.

The baptismal font is the return to the womb of conscious-ness, since consciousness has arisen in that state. The return to such a condition has healing value, because it brings things back to their origin, where nothing is disturbed, yet everything is still right. It is as if one were gaining there a sort of orientation of how things really ought to be.

Carl Jung

B UT the Christian is precisely the one who knows that the true reality of the world—of *this* world, of *this* life of ours—not of some mysterious "other" world—is in Christ; the Christian knows, rather, that Christ *is* this reality. In its self-sufficiency the world and all that exists in it has no meaning. And as long as we live after the fashion of this world, as long, in other words, as we make our life an end in itself, no meaning and no goal stand, for they are dissolved in death. It is only when we give up freely, totally, unconditionally, the self-sufficiency of our life, when we put all its meaning in Christ, that the "newness of life"—which means a new possession of the world—is given to us. The world then truly becomes the sacrament of Christ's presence, the growth of the Kingdom and of life eternal. For Christ, "being raised from the dead, dies no more; death has no more dominion over him." Baptism is thus the death of our selfishness and self-sufficiency, and it is the "likeness of Christ's death" because *Christ's death* is this unconditional self-surrender. And as Christ's death "trampled down death" because in it the ultimate meaning and strength of life were revealed, so also does our dying with him unite us with the new "life in God."

Alexander
Schmemann

M ORE was involved in the bathing process then, and hence more was implied in the bathing metaphor when used by antique authors, than is the case today. While one obviously could wash without bathing as one could eat without dining, both acts took on vastly enriched social and personal importance as they were ritualized, becoming freighted with more than merely utilitarian meaning in the process. The surviving Roman baths found throughout the Mediterranean area, Europe, and the Middle East testify to this. The New Testament corpus brings both this social pattern and the religious washing and bathing patterns found in Judaism to bear as it seeks to express what adherence to Christ in the Spirit means for Christian faith and practice. Receiving the Spirit through Christ is likened to a *birth bath*

in John 3:3–5 and Titus 3:5–7; to a *funeral bath* and burial
in Romans 6:1–11; to a bride's *nuptial bath* in Ephesians
5:26. These cultural practices were consummated in anointing and in arraying the body in clean, new, or otherwise
special clothing (Galatians 3:27) as the final stages of the
bath itself.   Aidan Kavanagh

DAY 46

THEN will I go in to the altar of God, the God of my
gladness and joy.

TAKE up the sword of the Spirit. Let your heart be an altar.
Then, with full confidence in God, present your body
for sacrifice. God desires not death, but faith; God thirsts not
for blood but for self-surrender; God is appeased not by   Peter Chrysologus
slaughter, but by the offering of your free will.   Fifth century

I wash my hands in innocence,
and I go around your altar, O LORD,
Giving voice to my thanks
    and recounting all your wondrous deeds.
O LORD, I love the house in which you dwell,
    the tenting-place of your glory.   Psalm 26:6–8

L OOK with favor on these offerings
and accept them as once you accepted
the gifts of your servant Abel,
the sacrifice of Abraham, our father in faith,
and the bread and wine offered by your priest
Eucharistic Prayer I   Melchisedech.

T HE letter to the Hebrews in the New Testament goes to
great length to point out that Christians offer no sacrifices because it is their conviction that none are needed. To
their mind, the death and resurrection of Jesus terminated
whatever usefulness might once have come from sacrifices
based on slaughter, the theft of life.

For those who follow Jesus, authentic sacrifice does not
involve the publicly sanctioned snatching of the life of
another to protect my life. It is not a matter of "someone else
must die so that I can live." Sacrifice is rather the gift of my
life for the life of the world. Sacrifice in the model Jesus
proposes means, "I spend myself so that others may live."

If the truth is that the eucharist is, above all else, a sacrifice,
the whole truth is that it takes two—Christ and the church—
to have that sacrifice sacramentally present. What if the
church comes unprepared to the occasion? In the third
century, the North African bishop, Cyprian, wrote once to
reprimand a wealthy woman in his church who made no
offering of her resources for the care of the poor but who
presumed nevertheless to show up at the communion table.
From Cyprian's perspective, the poor and rich alike must
spend themselves for others. This is the concrete self-gift of
Mary Collins   the church, the gift celebrated in the eucharist.

Y OU yourselves shall be named priests of the LORD.

J ESUS Christ is the high priest of our offerings,
our protector and helper in our weakness.
Through him we fix our gaze on the heavenly heights.
Through him we see as in a mirror
the pure and lofty face of God.
Through him the eyes of our heart have been opened.
Through him our foolish and darkened mind
grows up again into the light.
Through him the Master willed
that we should taste immortal knowledge.

Clement of Rome
First century

C OME, Almighty, to deliver;
Let us all thy life receive;
Suddenly return, and never,
Nevermore thy temples leave.
Thee we would be always blessing,
Serve thee as thy hosts above,
Pray, and praise thee without ceasing,
Glory in thy perfect love.

Finish then thy new creation,
Pure and spotless let us be;
Let us see thy great salvation
Perfectly restored in thee!
Changed from glory into glory,
Till in heav'n we take our place,
Till we cast our crowns before thee,
Lost in wonder, love, and praise.

Charles Wesley
Eighteenth century

F OR we do not have a high priest who is unable to
sympathize with our weaknesses, but one who has
similarly been tested in every way, yet without sin. So let us
confidently approach the throne of grace to receive mercy
and to find grace for timely help.

Hebrews 4:15–16

A S kingfishers catch fire, dragonflies draw flame;
As tumbled over rim in roundy wells
  Stones ring; like each tucked string tells, each hung
    bell's
Bow swung finds tongue to fling out broad its name;
Each mortal thing does one thing and the same:
  Deals out that being indoors each one dwells;
  Selves—goes itself; *myself* it speaks and spells,
Crying *What I do is me: for that I came.*

I say more: the just man justices;
  Keeps gráce: thát keeps all his goings graces;
Acts in God's eye what in God's eye he is—
  Chríst. For Christ plays in ten thousand places,
Lovely in limbs, and lovely in eyes not his
  To the Father through the features of men's faces.

*Gerard Manley
Hopkins
Nineteenth century*

O N praying with open, outstretched hands: On one
occasion I gained new insight into this ancient ges-
ture, when I read somewhere that the Assyrians had a word
for prayer which meant "to open the fist." The fist, and
especially a fist raised threateningly, is the sign of a high-
handed, even violent person. People grasp things in closed
hands when they are unwilling to let go of them; they use
clenched fists to assault and hurt and, even worse, to beat
others down so that they cannot get up.

Those who pray, however, are saying before God that they
are renouncing all highhandedness, all pride in their own

sufficiency, all violence. They open their fists. They hold up their empty hands to God: "I have nothing that I have not received from you, nothing that you have not placed in my empty hands. Therefore I do not keep a frantic hold on anything you have given me; therefore, too, I desire not to strike and hurt but only to give and to spread happiness and joy. For I myself am dependent on him who fills my empty hands with his gifts."

Balthasar Fischer

W HAT we commemorate before Easter is what we experience in this life; what we celebrate after Easter points to something we do not yet possess. This is why we keep the first season with fasting and prayer; but now the fast is over and we devote the present season to praise. Such is the meaning of the Alleluia we sing.

We are praising God now, assembled as we are here in church; but when we go our various ways again, it seems as if we cease to praise God. But provided we do not cease to live a good life, we shall always be praising God. You cease to praise God only when you swerve from justice and from what is pleasing to God. If you never turn aside from the good life, your tongue may be silent but your actions will cry aloud, and God will perceive your intentions; for as our ears hear each other's voices, so do God's ears hear our thoughts.

Augustine
Fourth century

DAY 48

I N the daytime the cloud of the LORD was seen over the Dwelling. Whereas at night, fire was seen in the cloud.

N OW you say, "How shall I proceed to think of God as he is in himself?" To this I can only reply, "I do not know."

With this question you bring me into the very darkness and cloud of unknowing that I want you to enter. A man may know completely and ponder thoroughly every created thing and its works, yes, and God's works, too, but not God himself. Thought cannot comprehend God. And so, I prefer to abandon all I can know, choosing rather to love him whom I cannot know. Though we cannot know him we can love him. By love he may be touched and embraced, never by thought. Of course, we do well at times to ponder God's majesty or kindness for the insight these meditations may bring. But in the real contemplative work you must set all this aside and cover it over with a cloud of forgetting. Then let your loving desire, gracious and devout, step bravely and joyfully beyond it and reach out to pierce the darkness above.

The Cloud of
Unknowing
Fourteenth century

H AVE you entered the storehouse of the snow,
and seen the treasury of the hail
Which I have reserved for times of stress,
    for the days of war and of battle?
Which way to the parting of the winds,
    whence the east wind spreads over the earth?
Who has laid out a channel for the downpour
    and for the thunderstorm a path
To enrich the waste and desolate ground
    till the desert blooms with verdure?
Has the rain a father;
    or who has begotten the drops of dew?
Out of whose womb comes the ice,
    and who gives the hoarfrost its birth in the skies,
When the waters lie covered as though with stone

that holds captive the surface of the deep?
Have you fitted a curb to the Pleiades,
    or loosened the bonds of Orion?
Can you bring forth the Mazzaroth in their season,
    or guide the Bear with its train?
Do you know the ordinances of the heavens;
    can you put into effect their plan on the earth?
Can you raise your voice among the clouds,
    or veil yourself in the waters of the storm?
Can you send forth the lightnings on their way,
    or will they say to you, "Here we are"?
Who counts the clouds in his wisdom?
    Or who tilts the water jars of heaven
So that the dust of earth is fused into a mass
    and its clods made solid?

                                                              Job 38:22–25, 27–38

WHENEVER a real "cloud of incense" rises from the censer (rarely enough, alas!), those present instinctively grasp the signification. The psalmist expressed it back in the Old Testament: "Let my prayer be counted like incense before thee" (Psalm 141:2). For example, the cloud of incense that envelops the altar and gifts at Mass and, in subsequent incensations, the priest and faithful as well, is a symbol of that atmosphere of prayer to which reference is made in the ancient summons spoken by the celebrant at the threshold of the inner sanctuary of the eucharist: *Sursum corda!* Lift up your hearts! Nothing is more important for the success of our liturgy than that we disentangle ourselves from the thicket of thoughts and cares which hold us prisoner, and make ourselves free for God. Symbolic human language in this area is based on the image of above and below, and no sign can give such simple and effective expression as incense does to the upward movement of adoration.

                                                              Balthasar Fischer

O N the morning of the third day there were peals of thunder and lightning, and a heavy cloud over the mountain, and a very loud trumpet blast, so that all the people in the camp trembled. But Moses led the people out of the camp to meet God, and they stationed themselves at the foot of the mountain. Mount Sinai was all wrapped in smoke, for the LORD came down upon it in fire. The smoke rose from it as though from a furnace, and the whole mountain trembled violently. The trumpet blast grew louder and louder, while Moses was speaking and God answering him with thunder.

Exodus 19:16–19

DAY 49

A LL you winds, bless the Lord.
Fire and heat, bless the Lord.

I have come to set the earth on fire, and how I wish it were already blazing! There is a baptism with which I must be baptized, and how great is my anguish until it is accomplished!

Luke 12:49–50

M EANWHILE Moses was tending the flock of his father-in-law Jethro, the priest of Midian. Leading the flock across the desert, he came to Horeb, the mountain of God. There an angel of the LORD appeared to him in fire flaming out of a bush. As he looked on, he was surprised to see that the bush, though on fire, was not consumed. So Moses decided, "I must go over to look at this remarkable sight, and see why the bush is not burned."

When the LORD saw him coming over to look at it more closely, God called out to him from the bush, "Moses! Moses!" He answered, "Here I am." God said, "Come no nearer! Remove the sandals from your feet, for the place where you stand is holy ground." Exodus 3:1–5

E VERY time I feel the Spirit moving in my heart,
  I will pray.
Yes, every time I feel the Spirit moving in my heart,
I will pray.

  Upon the mountain my Lord spoke,
  Out of his mouth came fire and smoke.

  Jordan river, chilly and cold,
  Chills the body but not the soul.

Afro-American
spiritual

Y OU are a fire always burning but never consuming; you
  are a fire consuming in your heat all the soul's selfish love; you are a fire lifting all chill and giving light. In your light you have made me know your truth. You are that light beyond all light who gives the mind's eye supernatural light in such fullness and perfection that you bring clarity even to the light of faith. In that faith I see that my soul has life, and in that light receives you who are Light.

Catherine of Siena
Fourteenth century

N EBUCHADNEZZAR flew into a rage and sent for Shadrach, Meshach, and Abednego, who were promptly
brought before the king. King Nebuchadnezzar questioned
them: "Is it true, Shadrach, Meshach, and Abednego, that
you will not serve my god, or worship the golden statue that I
set up? Be ready now to fall down and worship the statue I
had made, whenever you hear the sound of the trumpet,
flute, lyre, harp, psaltery, bagpipe, and all the other musical
instruments; otherwise, you shall be instantly cast into the
white-hot furnace, and who is the God that can deliver you
out of my hands?" Shadrach, Meshach, and Abednego
answered King Nebuchadnezzar, "There is no need for us to
defend ourselves before you in this matter. If our God, whom
we serve, can save us from the white-hot furnace and from
your hands, O king, may [God] save us! But even if [God]
will not, know, O king, that we will not serve your god or
worship the golden statue which you set up."

Nebuchadnezzar's face became livid with utter rage against
Shadrach, Meshach, and Abednego. He ordered the furnace to be heated seven times more than usual and had
some of the strongest men in his army bind Shadrach,
Meshach, and Abednego and cast them into the white-hot
furnace.

But the angel of the Lord went down into the furnace with
[the three young men], drove the fiery flames out of the
furnace, and made the inside of the furnace as though a
dew-laden breeze were blowing through it. The fire in no
way touched them or caused them pain or harm. Then these
three in the furnace with one voice sang, glorifying and
blessing God.

Daniel 3:13–20,
49–51

H E who saved the three young men in the furnace
became incarnate and suffered as a mortal man.
Through his sufferings he clothed what is mortal in the robe
of immortality.

Ode
Orthodox liturgy

N ONE other Lamb, none other Name,
None other Hope in heaven or earth or sea,
None other Hiding-place from guilt and shame,
  None beside Thee.

My faith burns low, my hope burns low,
  Only my heart's desire cries out in me
By the deep thunder of its want and woe,
  Cries out to Thee.

Lord, Thou art Life tho' I be dead,
  Love's Fire Thou art, however cold I be:
Nor heaven have I, nor place to lay my head,
  Nor home, but Thee.   Christina G. Rossetti

O ardent fire of my God, which contains, produces, and
imprints those living ardours which attract the humid
waters of my soul, and dry up the torrents of earthly delights,
and afterwards soften my hard self-opinionatedness, which
time has hardened so exceedingly! O consuming fire, which
even amid ardent flames imparts sweetness and peace to the
soul! In thee, and in none other, do we receive this grace of
being reformed to the image and likeness in which we were
created. O burning furnace, in which we enjoy the true
vision of peace, which tries and purifies the gold of the elect,
and leads the soul to seek eagerly for its highest good, even   Gertrude the Great
thyself, in thy eternal truth.   Thirteenth century

C OME, Holy Spirit, fill the hearts of your faithful.
And kindle in them the fire of your love.

Send forth your Spirit and they shall be created.
And you will renew the face of the earth.   Roman rite

H OLY breathing of God,
  I feel You stirring.

Warmed by this breath good things start to grow.
Even in strong, wealthy lands
fresh, mobilizing calls evoke planetary piety,
winning the hearts and the hands of the caring:
each in her chosen path,
each with a special gift,
take their stand
to create a world more fit for living,
Dom Helder Camara   more just and more humane.

T HE wind blows where it wills, and you can hear the
  sound it makes, but you do not know where it comes
from or where it goes; so it is with everyone who is born of
John 3:8   the Spirit.

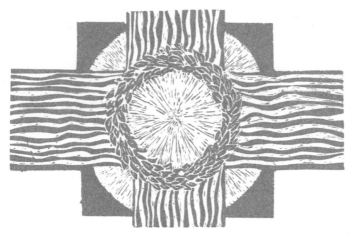

PENTECOST

I saw a new Jerusalem, the holy city, coming down out of heaven from God.

YOU shall count off seven weeks, computing them from the day when the sickle is first put to the standing grain. You shall then keep the feast of Weeks in honor of the LORD, your God, and the measure of your own freewill offering shall be in proportion to the blessing the LORD, your God, has bestowed on you. In the place which the LORD, your God, chooses as the dwelling place of [the LORD'S] name, you shall make merry in his presence together with your son and daughter, your male and female slave, and the Levite who belongs to your community, as well as the alien, the orphan and the widow among you.

Deuteronomy 16:9–11

WHEN the time for Pentecost was fulfilled, they were all in one place together. And suddenly there came from the sky a noise like a strong driving wind, and it filled the entire house in which they were. Then there appeared to them tongues as of fire, which parted and came to rest on each one of them. And they were all filled with the holy Spirit and began to speak in different tongues, as the Spirit enabled them to proclaim.

Now there were devout Jews from every nation under heaven staying in Jerusalem. At this sound, they gathered in a large crowd, but they were confused because each one heard them speaking in his own language. They were astounded, and in amazement they asked, "Are not all these people who are speaking Galileans? Then how does each of us hear them in his own native language? We are Parthians, Medes, and Elamites, inhabitants of Mesopotamia, Judea and Cappadocia, Pontus and Asia, Phrygia and Pamphylia, Egypt and the districts of Libya near Cyrene, as well as travelers from Rome, both Jews and converts to Judaism, Cretans and Arabs, yet we hear them speaking in our own tongues of the mighty acts of God."

Acts 2:1–11

WAKE, O wake, and sleep no longer,
For he who calls you is no stranger:
Awake, God's own Jerusalem!
Hear, the midnight bells are chiming
The signal for his royal coming:
Let voice to voice announce his name!
We feel his footsteps near,
The Bridegroom at the door—
Alleluia!
The lamps will shine
With light divine
As Christ the savior comes to reign.

Zion hears the sound of singing;
Our hearts are thrilled with sudden longing:

She stirs, and wakes, and stands prepared.
Christ, her friend, and lord, and lover,
Her star and sun and strong redeemer—
At last his mighty voice is heard.
The Son of God has come
To make with us his home:
Sing Hosanna!
The fight is won,
The feast begun:
We fix our eyes on Christ alone.

Glory, glory, sing the angels,
While music sounds from strings and cymbals;
All humankind, with songs arise!
Twelve the gates into the city,
Each one a pearl of shining beauty;
The streets of gold ring out with praise.
All creatures round the throne
Adore the holy One
With rejoicing:
Amen be sung
By ev'ry tongue
To crown their welcome to the King.

Philipp Nicolai
Sixteenth century

G OD'S city: that image has long gathered to itself massive human hopes. Would that there were a city, with
all the intensity and vigor of the great cities that have
centered human life and attracted human imagination and
made order out of the human experience of geography, but
now whole, sheltering and welcoming all, healing, luminous with God's presence, with the Spirit of God.

Such a city would be where God dwells.

Well, say Augustine and Luther and much of the Christian
tradition, to taste the meal is already to find oneself entering

into the city. The exchange of the meal—we bring wretch-edness and are given blessedness—is the commerce of the city.

But is it for us?

Come to the table. The gift of the meal is the word of Christ—"My body, my blood for you"—which may be kept, kept in the heart, held, the risen one still speaking there. Those who receive it become the very dwelling place of God. Where God dwells there is the city. Eat and drink. In the visible word which is the bread and cup, you are gathered with all the redeemed little ones into the city of the Lamb.

Gordon Lathrop

THE death of Jesus was not the end of his power and presence, for he was raised up by the power of God. Nor did it mark the end of the disciples' union with him. After Jesus had appeared to them and when they received the gift of the Spirit, they became apostles of the good news to the ends of the earth. In the face of poverty and persecution they transformed human lives and formed communities which became signs of the power and presence of God. Sharing in this same resurrection faith, contemporary followers of Christ can face the struggles and challenges that await those who bring the gospel vision to bear on our complex eco-nomic and social world.

Economic Justice for All

HOLY Spirit, Lord divine,
Come, from heights of heav'n and shine,
  Come with blessed radiance bright!
Come, O Father of the poor,
Come, whose treasured gifts endure,
  Come, our heart's unfailing light!

Of consolers, wisest, best,
And our souls' most welcome guest,
  Sweet refreshment, sweet repose.
In our labor rest most sweet,
Pleasant coolness in the heat,
  Consolation in our woes.

Light most blessed, shine with grace
In our heart's most secret place,
  Fill your faithful through and through!
Left without your presence here,
Life itself would disappear,
  Nothing thrives apart from you!

Cleanse our soiled hearts of sin,
Arid souls refresh within,
  Wounded lives to health restore!
Bend the stubborn heart and will,
Melt the frozen, warm the chill,
  Guide the wayward home once more!

On the faithful who are true
And profess their faith in you,
  In your sev'n-fold gift descend!
Give us virtue's sure reward,
Give us your salvation, Lord,
  Give us joys that never end!
Amen. Alleluia!

Sequence
Twelfth century

F OR fifty days after Easter it is granted to us to live in the paschal joy, to experience time as the *feast*. And then comes the "last and great" day of Pentecost and with it our *return* into the real time of this world. At Vespers of that day the Christians are ordered—for the first time since Easter—*to kneel*. The night is approaching, the night of time and history, of the daily effort, of the fatigue and temptations, of the whole inescapable burden of life.

Alexander
Schmemann

T HE inner nature of the church is now made known to us in various images. Taken either from the life of the shepherd or from cultivation of the land, from the art of building or from family life and marriage, these images have their preparation in the books of the prophets.

The church is, accordingly, a sheepfold, the sole and necessary gateway to which is Christ. It is also a flock, whose sheep, although watched over by human shepherds, are nevertheless at all times led and brought to pasture by Christ himself, the Good Shepherd and prince of shepherds, who gave his life for his sheep.

The church is a cultivated field, the tillage of God. On that land the ancient olive tree grows whose holy roots were the prophets and in which the reconciliation of Jews and gentiles has been brought about and will be brought about again. That land, like a choice vineyard, has been planted by the heavenly cultivator.

Often, too, the church is called the building of God. This edifice has many names to describe it: the house of God in which God's family dwells; the household of God in the Spirit; the dwelling-place of God among humans; and, especially, the holy temple. This temple is compared in the liturgy to the Holy City, the New Jerusalem. As living stones we here on earth are built into it. It is this holy city that is seen by John as it comes down out of heaven from God when the world is made anew.

Constitution on the
Church, Vatican II

YOU, O Christ, are the Kingdom of Heaven;
    You, the land promised to the gentle;
You, the grazing lands of paradise;
You, the hall of the
    celestial banquet;
You, the ineffable marriage chamber;
You, the table set for all;
You, the bread of life;
You, the unheard of drink;
You, both the urn for the water and the life giving water;
You, moreover, the inextinguishable lamp for each one
    of the saints;
You, the garment and the crown and the one who
    distributes the crowns;
You, the joy and rest; You, the delight and glory;
You, the gaiety; You, the mirth;
and your grace, grace of the Spirit of all sanctity,
    will shine like the sun in all the saints;
and You, inaccessible sun, will shine in their midst
    and all will shine brightly,
to the degree of their faith, their asceticism,
their hope and their love,
their purification and their illumination by your Spirit.

Symeon the
New Theologian
Eleventh century

HOPE, Life, Way, Salvation, Understanding,
Wisdom, Light,
Judge, Door, Most High, King, Precious Stone,
     Prophet, Priest,
Messiah, Sabaoth, Teacher, Spouse, Mediator,
Scepter, Dove, Hand, Stone, Son, and Emmanuel,
Vineyard, Shepherd, Sheep, Peace, Root, Vine-stock,
Olive Tree, Source, Wall, Lamb, Victim, Lion, Intercessor,
Word, Man, Net, Rock, House:
     Christ Jesus is everything.

Damasus
Fourth century

An Order for Daily Prayer

- ## Call to prayer

    For morning:
    This is the day that the Lord has made, alleluia;
    let us rejoice and be glad in it, alleluia.

    For midday:
    Since you have been raised to life with Christ, alleluia;
    seek the things that are above, alleluia.

    For evening:
    Abide with us, Lord, for it is evening, alleluia;
    and the day is almost over, alleluia.

Morning remembrance of baptism

Dip your hand in water and make the sign of the cross.

Evening candle lighting

Light an Easter candle to welcome the evening while saying:
Jesus Christ is the light of the world.

Psalm

Option 1, Psalm 148

Praise the Lord! Hallelujah!
Praise God from the sky,
   Praise God from the heights;
Praise God, all you angels,
   Praise God, heaven's armies.
Praise God, sun and moon,
   Praise God, all bright stars;
Praise God, skies above,
   And waters above the skies.
They praise their true Lord,
   Who ordered their making,
Who placed them for ever
   In the courses they follow.

Praise the Lord from the earth,
   Ocean deeps and dragons,
Fire and hail, snow and smoke,
   Gale wind doing God's word;
All mountains and hills,
   All fruit trees and cedars,
All beasts, wild or tame,
   Creeping things and soaring birds;
All earth's kings and peoples,
   All earth's princes and rulers,
Young women and men,
   And the old with the young,
Praise the name of the Lord;
   God alone is worthy of honor.
God's might is above earth and sky;
   God's people rise up in power.
Israel's children are close to God,
   God the glory of all faithful people!
Praise the Lord! Hallelujah!

Option 2, Psalm 23

Lord, my shepherd, there's nothing I lack.
   In fresh pastures you let me lie down;
You lead me beside quiet waters;
   You restore me to life.
In order to show who you are,
   You guide me in paths that are right.
Even walking through dark valleys,
   I have no fear of harm.
For you yourself are with me;
   Your rod and staff reassure me.

Right in front of my foes,
   You lay out a feast for me.
You anoint my head with oil;
   My cup is overflowing.

Goodness and love pursue me
   Every day of my life;
God's house will be my home
   As long as I may live.

Option 3, Psalm 114 (page 8)

■ Verse of the day

Read the short scripture verse at the head of the proper day.

■ Meditation

Read one more of the texts for the proper day.

Silence

Canticle

For morning:
Blessed are you, O Lord, the God of Israel!
You have come to your people and set them free.
You have raised up for us a horn of deliverance
    in the house of your servant David.
Through the mouth of your holy prophets of old
you promised liberation from our enemies,
from the hands of all who hate us.

You promised to show mercy to our forebears
and to remember your holy covenant.
This was the oath you swore to our father Abraham:
that, rescued from the hands of our enemies,
we are free to worship you without fear,
holy and righteous in your sight
all the days of our life.

You, my child, shall be called the prophet of the Most High,
for you will go before the Lord to prepare the way,
to give God's people knowledge of salvation
    by the forgiveness of their sins.
In the tender compassion of our God
the morning sun will break upon us,
to shine on those who dwell in darkness
    and the shadow of death,
and to guide our feet in the way of peace.

Luke 1:68–79

For evening:
My soul magnifies the Lord,
and my spirit rejoices in God my Savior
who has looked with favor on me, a lowly serving maid.
From this day all generations will call me blessed.

The Mighty One has done great things for me:
holy the name of the Lord,
whose mercy is on the God-fearing
from generation to generation.
The arm of the Lord is filled with strength,

scattering the proudhearted.
God cast the mighty from their thrones,
lifting up the lowly.
God filled the hungry with good things,
sending the rich away empty.

God has come to the help of Israel, the Lord's servant,
remembering mercy,
the mercy promised to our forebears,
to Abraham and his children for ever.

Luke 1:46–55

Intercessions and Lord's Prayer

*Pray in Jesus' name for the world, the poor, the church, our
neighbors, friends, family and ourselves. At the end, all the prayers
are sealed with the Lord's Prayer.*

■ Prayer for the week

Days 1 to 7:
O God, our light, our beauty, our rest:
in the resurrection of your Son
you have brought us into your new creation.
Form us into your people,
and order our lives in you
through Christ our Lord. Amen. Alleluia.

Days 8 to 14:
O God, our bread, our milk and our honey:
in the resurrection of your Son
you have brought us to your table.
Feed us with your plenty,
and enlarge our table for all the hungry
through Christ our Lord. Amen. Alleluia.

Days 15 to 21:
O God, our rainbow, our dove, our promised land:
in the resurrection of your Son
you have brought us into your ark.
Protect us from storm,

and ferry us to your welcoming shore
through Christ our Lord. Amen. Alleluia.

Days 22 to 28:
O God, our shepherd, our gate, our lamb:
in the resurrection of your Son
you have brought us into your pasture.
Guide us to your clear streams,
and tame the wolf at our gate
through Christ our Lord. Amen. Alleluia.

Days 29 to 35:
O God, our grove, our lover, our well:
in the resurrection of your Son
you have brought us into your garden.
Marry us for now and for ever,
and give us to eat from the tree of life
through Christ our Lord. Amen. Alleluia.

Days 36 to 42:
O God, our sovereign, our banquet, our crown:
in the resurrection of your Son
you have brought us into your palace.
Train us to be heirs to your throne,
that we may shield the needy
through Christ our Lord. Amen. Alleluia.

Days 43 to 49:
O God, Holy One, our altar, our cloud:
in the resurrection of your Son
you have brought us into your temple.
Accept the sacrifices we offer,
and draw us into the fire of your Spirit
through Christ our Lord. Amen. Alleluia.

Day 50:
O God,
when all things come to their end,
you bring us into the city of the resurrection of your Son.
Shelter every nation and tongue with your Spirit,
and feed us all with joy unending
through Christ our Lord. Amen. Alleluia.

Endnotes

First Week of Easter

DAY 1

The light: John 1:5.

Christ is risen: From *Pascha: The Resurrection of Christ*. Published by St. Vladimir's Seminary Press, 1980. Used with permission.

Flame, which: From *Sacred Signs* by Romano Guardini with permission from the publisher, Michael Glazier, Inc., Wilmington.

O Splendor: Text copyright ©1978 *Lutheran Book of Worship*. Reprinted by permission of Augsburg Publishing House.

The people say: From *The Time of the Spirit*, readings selected and edited by George Every, Richard Harries and Kallistos Ware. Published by St. Vladimir's Seminary Press, 1984. Used with permission.

O Light Invisible: From "Choruses from 'The Rock'" in *Collected Poems 1909–1962* by T. S. Eliot. Copyright ©1936, Harcourt Brace Jovanovich, Inc.; copyright ©1963, 1964 by T. S. Eliot. Reprinted with permission of the publisher.

It is on Sunday: From *Springtime of the Liturgy* by Lucien Deiss, translated by Matthew J. O'Connell. Copyright ©1979, The Order of St. Benedict, Inc. Published by The Liturgical Press, Collegeville MN. Used with permission.

DAY 2

You fixed: Psalm 104:5.

So it is: From *To Dance with God: Family Ritual and Community Celebration* by Gertrud Mueller Nelson. Copyright ©1986, Gertrud Mueller Nelson. Published by Paulist Press, New York, 1986. Used with permission.

DAY 3

Then shall: Psalm 96:12.

O God: From *Heart of Prayer: African, Jewish and Biblical Prayers*, edited by Anthony J. Gittins, CSSp. Published by Collins Publishers, London, 1985.

What a glorious: From *The Church's Year of Grace* by Pius Parsch. Copyright ©1954, The Order of St. Benedict, Inc. Published by The Liturgical Press, Collegeville MN. Used with permission.

A tree: From *New Seeds of Contemplation* by Thomas Merton. Copyright ©1961, The Abbey of Gethsemani, Inc. Reprinted by permission of New Directions Publishing Corp.

It is impossible: From *Jesus in Focus: A Life in Its Setting* by Gerard S. Sloyan. Copyright ©1983, Gerard S. Sloyan. Published by Twenty-Third Publications, Mystic CT.

O that I had: Music can be found in *Worship* #546, *The Lutheran Hymnal* #243, and *Lutheran Book of Worship* #560.

DAY 4

Yours is: Psalm 74:16.

Sunrise is: From *Conjectures of a Guilty Bystander* by Thomas Merton. Copyright ©1965, 1966, The Abbey of Gethsemani. Reprinted with permission of Doubleday, a division of Bantam, Doubleday, Dell Publishing Group.

The spacious: Paraphrase of Psalm 19. Music can be found in *The Hymnal 1982* #409.

Most High: From *The Little Flowers of St. Francis*, translated by Raphael Brown. Copyright ©1958, Beverly H. Brown. Used by permission of Doubleday, a division of Bantam, Doubleday, Dell Publishing Group.

Christ, whose glory: Music can be found in *Lutheran Book of Worship* #265.

It is an unusual: *Signs, Words, and Gestures* by Balthasar Fischer. Copyright ©1981, Pueblo Publishing Company, Inc. Used with permission.

DAY 5

Praise the: Psalm 148:7, 10.

After the: From *Tales of the Hasidim, The Early Masters* by Martin Buber, translated by Olga Marx Perlzweig. Copyright ©1947, Schocken Books. Published by Pantheon Books, a division of Random House, Inc. Used with permission.

(sitting in a tree-): Copyright ©1940 by E. E. Cummings; renewed 1968 by Marion Morehouse Cummings. Reprinted from *Complete Poems 1913–1962* by E. E. Cummings by permission of Harcourt Brace Jovanovich, Inc.

The world: From *The Poems of Gerard Manley Hopkins*, fourth edition, edited by W. H. Gardner and N. H. MacKenzie. Published by Oxford University Press.

The whole bright world: Music can be found in *The Oxford Book of Carols* #96.

Day 6

In wisdom: Psalm 104:24.

Thou mastering me: From *The Poems of Gerard Manley Hopkins*, fourth edition, edited by W. H. Gardner and N. H. MacKenzie. Published by Oxford University Press.

A Hasidic story: From *Messengers of God, Biblical Portraits and Legends* by Elie Wiesel. Published by Summit Books, a division of Simon and Schuster, New York, 1976. Used with permission.

Day 7

Only in God: Psalm 62:2.

The meaning: From *The Sabbath, Its Meaning for Modern Man* by Abraham Joshua Heschel. Copyright ©1951, Abraham Joshua Heschel copyright © renewed 1979, Abraham Joshua Heschel. Reprinted by permission of Farrar, Straus and Giroux, Inc., New York.

O Lord God: From *The Confessions of St. Augustine*, translated by John K. Ryan. Copyright ©1960, Doubleday and Company, Inc. Reprinted with permission of Doubleday, a division of Bantam, Doubleday, Dell Publishing Group.

The Lord: From *The Revelations of Divine Love of Julian of Norwich*, Anthony Clarke Books, Wheathampstead-Hertfordshire.

Holla: "The Shout" by Adam Fox from *Carols of Today*. Copyright ©1965, Oxford University Press. Reprinted with permission.

Second Week of Easter

Day 8

Taste and see: Psalm 34:9.

The table fellowship: From *Life Together* by Dietrich Bonhoeffer, translated by John W. Doberstein. Harper and Row Publishers.

One of the brethren: From *Early Dominicans, Selected Writings* edited by Simon Tugwell, OP. From the Classics of Western Spirituality Series. Copyright ©1982, Missionary Society of St. Paul the Apostle in the State of New York. Used by permission of Paulist Press.

By this light: From *The Prayers of Catherine of Siena* edited by Suzanne Noffke. Copyright ©1983. Used by permission of Paulist Press.

The table is: From *The Humanity of Man* by Edmond Barbotin, translated by Matthew J. O'Connell. Copyright ©1975, Orbis Books, Maryknoll NY. Used with permission.

Day 9

God's bread: John 6:33.

We had: By *Little and By Little, The Selected Writings of Dorothy Day*, edited by Robert Ellsberg. Published by Alfred A. Knopf, Inc., New York, 1983. Used with permission.

Just as: *Luther's Works*, vol. 2, Lectures on Genesis Chapters 6–14, edited by Jaroslav Pelikan. Published by Fortress Press, Philadelphia PA. Used with permission.

In the act: From *The New York Times Bread and Soup Cookbook* by Yvonne Young Tarr. Copyright ©1972, Quadrangle Books, Inc. Reprinted by permission of Times Books, a division of Random House, Inc.

Now the green: Text copyright © Oxford University Press. Used with permission.

I am: From *Early Christian Prayers*, edited by A. Hamman, translated by Walter Mitchell. Published by Regnery Gateway, Inc. Used with permission.

Bread as: From *The Humanity of Man* by Edmond Barbotin, translated by Matthew J. O'Connell. Copyright ©1975, Orbis Books, Maryknoll NY. Used with permission.

Then let us: Music can be found in *Lutheran Book of Worship* #134.

Day 10

I am: John 15:1.

We were created: From *The Supper of the Lamb* by Robert Farrar Capon. Copyright ©1967, 1969, Robert Farrar Capon. Reprinted by permission of Doubleday, a division of Bantam, Doubleday, Dell Publishing Group.

It was with good reason: From *From the Fathers to the Churches, Daily Spiritual Readings,* edited by Brother Kenneth. Published by Collins Liturgical Publications, London, 1983.

You soul devoted to God: From *Bonaventure: The Tree of Life,* translated by Ewert Cousins. From the Classics of Western Spirituality Series. Copyright ©1978, Missionary Society of St. Paul the Apostle in the State of New York. Used by permission of Paulist Press.

Similarly: From *The Liturgy of the Hours.* Copyright ©1974, International Committee on English in the Liturgy, Inc. (ICEL). All rights reserved.

Paul cried: From *St. Cyril of Jerusalem's Lectures on the Christian Sacraments,* edited by F. L. Cross. Published by St. Vladimir's Seminary Press, 1977. Used with permission.

The wine: From *Bread in the Wilderness* by Thomas Merton. Copyright ©1971, The Order of St. Benedict, Inc. Published by The Liturgical Press, Collegeville MN. Used with permission.

But it is: From *The Liturgy of the Hours.* Copyright ©1974, International Committee on English in the Liturgy, Inc. (ICEL). All rights reserved.

DAY 11

I eat: Song of Songs 5:1.

Like an eagle: From *The Complete Bible, An American Translation.* University of Chicago Press, 1939; adapted.

The deacons: From *Springtime of the Liturgy* by Lucien Deiss, translated by Matthew J. O'Connell. Copyright ©1979, The Order of St. Benedict, Inc. Published by The Liturgical Press, Collegeville MN. Used with permission.

Why do you: From *Baptism,* edited by Andre Hamman. Published by Alba House, a division of the Society of St. Paul, Staten Island NY. Used with permission.

Jesus Christ: From *Early Christian Prayers,* edited by A. Hamman, translated by Walter Mitchell. Published by Regnery Gateway, Inc. Used with permission.

Now we're going: From the "I've Been to the Mountaintop" speech given by Martin Luther King, Jr. on April 3, 1963, Masonic Temple, Memphis TN.

I saw: From *Medieval Women's Visionary Literature,* edited by Elizabeth Alvilda Petroff. Copyright ©1986, Oxford University Press, Inc. Used with permission.

DAY 12

There is: John 1:29.

What wondrous love: From the collection *The Southern Harmony,* 1835, ascribed to Alexander Means. Music can be found in *Worship* #60, *Lutheran Book of Worship* #385, *The Hymnal 1982* #439.

"Brethren": From *The Sound and the Fury* by William Faulkner. Copyright ©1929 and renewed 1957, William Faulkner. Reprinted by permission of Random House, Inc.

At the Lamb's: Music can be found in *Worship* #459 and #460, *Lutheran Book of Worship* #210, *The Hymnal 1982* #174.

DAY 13

You must: John 13:14.

Let us come: From *Saint Ambrose, Theological and Dogmatic Works,* translated by Roy J. Deferrari. Published by The Catholic University of America Press in association with Consortium Books, Washington DC, 1963. Used with permission.

Because we have been: From *The Challenge of Peace: God's Promise and Our Response.* Copyright ©1983, United States Catholic Conference (USCC). Used with permission.

Lord God, your love: By Brian Wren. Copyright ©1977, Hope Publishing Company, Carol Stream IL. All rights reserved. Used with permission.

A Christian is: From *Christian Liberty* by Martin Luther, edited by Harold J. Grimm. Copyright ©1957, Fortress Press, Philadelphia PA. Used with permission.

DAY 14

You crushed: Psalm 74:14.

The Holy One: From *Jewish Symbols in the Greco-Roman Period,* vol. 5, Bollingen Series 37, by Erwin R. Goodenough. Published by Pantheon Books, a division of Random House, Inc. Bollingen Series by Princeton University Press, Princeton NJ.

We should: From *The Bible and the Liturgy* by Jean Danielou, SJ. Published by University of Notre Dame Press, 1956. Used with permission.

Ichthus-born: From *Early Christian Prayers,* edited by A. Hamman, translated by Walter Mitchell. Published by Regnery Gateway, Inc. Used with permission.

Third Week of Easter

DAY 15

Then God said: Genesis 8:15.

We turn to you: From *A Book of Prayers*. Copyright ©1982, International Committee on English in the Liturgy, Inc. (ICEL). All rights reserved.

The ark: From "The Mystic Magi" by Robert Stephen Hawker, 1803–1875. From *The Cherry Tree*, a collection of over 500 poems chosen by Geoffrey Origson, Vanguard Press NY, 1959. Copyright ©1959, Geoffrey Origson.

Although the winds: From *The Hymns of Ann Griffiths* by John Ryan, English translation by Robert O. F. Wynne and John Ryan. Published by Y Llyfrfa, Caernarfon.

DAY 16

Jesus sent: Mark 6:7.

He is the Way: From *W. H. Auden: Collected Poems*, edited by Edward Mendelson. Copyright ©1976, Edward Mendelson, William Meredith and Monroe K. Spears. Reprinted by permission of Random House, Inc.

DAY 17

Let not: Psalm 69:16.

Fresh from: From *Early Christian Prayers*, edited by A. Hamman, translated by Walter Mitchell. Published by Regnery Gateway, Inc. Used with permission.

This joyful Eastertide: Music can be found in *Lutheran Book of Worship* #149, *The Hymnal 1982* #192.

In the same: From *The Liturgy of the Hours*. Copyright ©1974, International Committee on English in the Liturgy, Inc. (ICEL). All rights reserved.

Temptation is like: From *St. Cyril of Jerusalem's Lectures on the Christian Sacraments*, edited by F. L. Cross. Published by St. Vladimir's Seminary Press, Crestwood NY, 1977. Used with permission.

He would let the world: From *Heart of the World* by Hans Urs von Balthasar, translated by Erasmo S. Leiva. Ignatius Press, San Francisco, 1979. Used with permission.

DAY 18

The song: Song of Songs 2:12.

For just as: From *The Ante-Nicene Fathers, Translations of the Writings of the Fathers Down to A.D. 325*, vol. II, edited by Alexander Roberts and James Donaldson. Published by William B. Eerdmans Publishing Co. Used with permission.

Rise, therefore: From *Bonaventure: The Tree of Life*, translated by Ewert Cousins. From the Classics of Western Spirituality Series. Copyright ©1978, Missionary Society of St. Paul the Apostle in the State of New York. Used by permission of the Paulist Press.

Whilst thou: From *Medieval Women's Visionary Literature*, edited by Elizabeth Alvilda Petroff. Copyright ©1986, Oxford University Press. Used with permission.

DAY 19

Like a green: Psalm 52:10.

Then when you were stripped: From *Documents of the Baptismal Liturgy* by E. C. Whitaker. Reproduced by permission of S.P.C.K., London.

The sign of Christ: From *Signs, Words, and Gestures* by Balthasar Fischer. Copyright ©1981, Pueblo Publishing Company, Inc. Used with permission.

Mary sings: From *Kontakia of Romanos, Byzantine Melodist. I: On the Person of Christ*, translated by Marjorie Carpenter. Copyright ©1970, the Curators of the University of Missouri. Used by permission of the University of Missouri Press.

Let us therefore: From *Springtime of the Liturgy* by Lucien Deiss, translated by Matthew J. O'Connell. Copyright ©1979, The Order of St. Benedict, Inc. Published by The Liturgical Press, Collegeville MN. Used with permission.

Ah, how good and lovely: From *The Psalms: A New Translation for Prayer and Worship* by Gary Chamberlain. Copyright ©1984, The Upper Room, reproduced herein by permission of the author. All rights reserved.

DAY 20

Then I saw: Revelation 21:1.

Though nature's strength: Music can be found in *Lutheran Book of Worship* #544.

O thou whose pow'r: From *A Treasury of Poems for Worship and Devotion*, edited by Charles L. Wallis. Harper and Row Publishers.

Christian communities: From *Economic Justice for All: Catholic Social Teaching and the U. S. Economy.* Copyright ©1986, United States Catholic Conference (USCC). Used with permission.

Day 21

Around the: Revelation 4:3.

Throughout Easter's fifty days: From "The Candle" by Patrick Regan. From *Easter, the Fifty Days.* Copyright © The Liturgical Conference, Washington DC. All rights reserved. Used with permission.

Noah, Noah: From the Chester Miracle Play "Noyes' Fludde," *English Miracle Plays, Moralities and Interludes,* edited by Alfred W. Pollard, Clarendon Press. Used with permission.

Yea, Truth: From "On the Morning of Christ's Nativity" by John Milton. From *The New Oxford Book of Christian Verse,* Oxford University Press, 1981.

Fourth Week of Easter

Day 22

Tell me: Song of Songs 1:7.

What are: From *From the Fathers to the Churches, Daily Spiritual Readings,* edited by Brother Kenneth. Published by Collins Liturgical Publications, London, 1983.

This sheep: From *Medieval Women's Visionary Literature,* edited by Elizabeth Alvilda Petroff. Copyright ©1986, Oxford University Press. Used with permission.

Spring has now: Based on two Easter carols, *Tempus adest floridum* and *In vernali tempore,* both from the collection *Piae Cantiones,* 1582.

Day 23

I am: John 10:14.

The king of love: Music can be found in *Worship* #609.

Shepherd of: Music can be found in *The Lutheran Hymnal* #628.

Once a young: From *The Poems of St. John of the Cross,* translated by John Frederick Nims. Copyright ©1959, John Frederick Nims. Used by permission of The University of Chicago Press.

Day 24

From your: Psalm 36:9.

The wise are servants: From *Kontakia of Romanos, Byzantine Melodist. II: On Christian Life,* translated by Marjorie Carpenter. Copyright ©1973, the Curators of the University of Missouri. Used by permission of the University of Missouri Press.

Shall we gather: Music can be found in *Lead Me, Guide Me* #103.

A small cup held: From *A Book of Uncommon Prayers* by Catherine de Vinck, 1976. Used by permission of the publishers, Alleluia Press, Allendale NJ.

As pants the hart: Music can be found in *Lutheran Book of Worship* #425.

Day 25

I am: John 10:7.

Many years ago: From *The Expository Times,* vol. 71, October 1959–September 1960, edited by A. W. Hastings and E. Hastings. Published by T. & T. Clark, Edinburgh, Scotland. Used with permission.

Because of sin: From *The Prayers of Catherine of Siena,* edited by Suzanne Noffke. Used by permission of Paulist Press.

Day 26

The wolf: Isaiah 65:25.

The fierce wolf: From *The Little Flowers of St. Francis,* translated by Raphael Brown. Copyright ©1958, Beverly H. Brown. Used by permission of Doubleday, a division of Bantam, Doubleday, Dell Publishing Group.

I refuse: From the Nobel Prize Acceptance Speech by Martin Luther King, Jr. on December 10, 1964, Oslo, Norway.

Ye choirs of new Jerusalem: Attributed to St. Fulbert of Chartres, eleventh century hymn *Chorae Novae Jerusalem,* translated by Robert Campbell, 1814–1868.

Day 27

Only when: Exodus 19:13.

The paschal lamb: Stanza 2 of "O Sorrow Deep," *The Hymnal 1982* #173.

On behalf of Isaac: From *Melito of Sardis on Pascha*. Texts and translations edited by Stuart George Hall, 1979. Published by The Clarendon Press, Oxford, England. Used with permission.

DAY 28

The Lamb: Revelation 7:17.

For the marriage: Revised Standard Version.

By the cross: From *The Liturgy of the Hours*. Copyright ©1974, International Committee on English in the Liturgy, Inc. (ICEL). All rights reserved.

Just as I am: Music can be found in *Lutheran Book of Worship* #296.

He is the Pascha: From *Melito of Sardis on Pascha*. Texts and translations edited by Stuart George Hall, 1979. Published by The Clarendon Press, Oxford, England. Used with permission.

Fifth Week of Easter

DAY 29

You shall: Isaiah 58:11.

After the anointing: From *Documents of the Baptismal Liturgy* by E.C. Whitaker. Used by permission of S.P.C.K., London.

The Lord into his garden's come: From the collection *The Repository of Sacred Music, Part Second*, edited by John Wyeth, Harrisburg PA, 1813.

DAY 30

You are: Song of Songs 4:12.

About half an hour later: From *The Last Battle* by C. S. Lewis. Used by permission of the estate of C. S. Lewis.

God to enfold me: From *Celtic Prayers*, selected by Avery Brooke from the collection of Alexander Carmichael. The Seabury Press, Harper and Row Publishers.

DAY 31

To the victor: Revelation 2:7.

I am yearning: From *The Hymns of Ann Griffiths*, edited by John Ryan. English translation by Robert O. F. Wynne and John Ryan. Published by Y Llyfrfa, Caernarfon.

And you, high eternal Trinity: From *The Prayers of Catherine of Siena*, edited by Suzanne Noffke. Used by permission of Paulist Press.

Those who gain: From *The Liturgy of the Hours*. Copyright ©1974, International Committee on English in the Liturgy, Inc. (ICEL). All rights reserved.

There in God's garden: Based on a Hungarian hymn by P. K. Imre, 1961, paraphrased by Erik Routley in *Westminister Praise*. Copyright ©1976, Hinshaw Music, Inc. Used with permission.

By thy cross: From *Pascha: The Resurrection of Christ*. Published by St. Vladimir's Seminary Press, 1980. Used with permission.

DAY 32

How beautiful: Song of Songs 7:7.

O eternal Father!: From *Catherine of Siena, The Dialogue*, translated by Suzanne Noffke. From the Classics of Western Spirituality Series. Copyright ©1980, Missionary Society of St. Paul the Apostle in the State of New York. Used by permission of Paulist Press.

While it is: From *The Poems of Emily Dickinson*, edited by Thomas H. Johnson. Reprinted by permission of the publishers. Copyright ©1951, 1955, 1979, 1983, the President and Fellows of Harvard College. Published by Harvard University Press, Cambridge MS.

As soon as they: From *Documents of the Baptismal Liturgy*, edited by E. G. Whitaker. Reproduced by permission of S.P.C.K., London.

According to a custom: *Signs, Words, and Gestures* by Balthasar Fischer. Copyright ©1981, Pueblo Publishing Company, Inc. Used with permission.

DAY 33

You will: John 15:10.

And so, now I call: *Kontakia of Romanos, Byzantine Melodist. II: On Christian Life*, translated by Marjorie Carpenter. Copyright ©1973, the Curators of the University of Missouri. Used by permission of the University of Missouri Press.

In her: From *Medieval Women's Visionary Literature*, edited by Elizabeth Alvilda Petroff. Copyright ©1986, Oxford University Press, Inc. Used with permission.

We the: From *Early Christian Prayers*, edited by A. Hamman, translated by Walter Mitchell. Published by Regnery Gateway, Inc. Used with permission.

When love is found: By Brian Wren. Copyright ©1983, Hope Publishing Company, Carol Stream IL. All rights reserved. Used with permission.

DAY 34

Refresh me: Song of Songs 2:5.

I speak: From *The Liturgy of the Hours,* Copyright ©1974, International Committee on English in the Liturgy (ICEL). All rights reserved.

Picture in your mind: From *Bonaventure: The Tree of Life,* translated by Ewert Cousins. From the Classics of Western Spirituality Series. Copyright ©1978, Missionary Society of St. Paul the Apostle in the State of New York. Used by permission of the Paulist Press.

Plantation of God: From *Springtime of the Liturgy* by Lucien Deiss, translated by Matthew J. O'Connell. Copyright ©1979, The Order of St. Benedict, Inc. Published by The Liturgical Press, Collegeville MN. Used with permission.

The church rejoices: From *Saint Ambrose, Theological and Dogmatic Works,* translated by Roy J. Deferrari. The Catholic University Press in association with Consortium Books, Washington DC, 1963. Used with permission.

The tree of life: Music can be found in the *Second Penguin Book of Christmas Carols,* edited by Elizabeth Poston.

DAY 35

You are: Song of Songs 4:15.

Someone was: From *The Story of My Life* by Helen Keller, 1918.

Sixth Week of Easter

DAY 36

Bring me: Song of Songs 1:4.

But one thing more: From *Baptism,* edited by Andre Hamman. Published by Alba House, a division of the Society of St. Paul, Staten Island NY. Used with permission.

Crown him with: Music can be found in *Lutheran Book of Worship* #170.

What if our God: From *Letters for God's Name* by Gail Ramshaw-Schmidt. The Seabury Press, Harper and Row Publishers.

"Unto Me?": From *The Complete Poems of Emily Dickinson,* edited by Thomas H. Johnson. Copyright ©1929 by Martha Dickinson Bianchi; copyright © renewed 1957 by Mary L. Hampson.

DAY 37

On the throne: Revelation 4:3.

Jerusalem the golden: Music can be found in *The Hymnal 1982* #624.

Holy Mary: From *A Book of Prayers.* Copyright ©1982, International Committee on English in the Liturgy (ICEL). All rights reserved.

He is King of kings: Music can be found in *Lead Me, Guide Me* #220.

Now glad of heart: Music can be found in the *Oxford Book of Carols* #95. Used by permission from Oxford University Press.

DAY 38

Wisdom has: Proverbs 9:2.

Join, then: From *Early Christian Prayers,* edited by A. Hamman, translated by Walter Mitchell. Published by Regnery Gateway, Inc. Used with permission.

Come away to the skies: From the collection *The Southern Harmony.* Music can be found in *The Hymnal 1982* #213.

DAY 39

This day: Psalm 2:7.

O Christ: "Freed" by Roger Schutz from *Eerdman's Book of Famous Prayers: A Treasury of Christian Prayers through the Centuries,* compiled by Veronica Zundel. Copyright ©, A. R. Mowbray and Co. Ltd, UK. Published by William B. Eerdmans Publishing Company, Grand Rapids MI.

First there: From *There Are Different Ministries* by Robert Hovda. Copyright ©1975, The Liturgical Conference, Washington DC. All rights reserved. Used with permission.

All of us: From *Economic Justice for All: Catholic Social Teaching and the U.S. Economy.* Copyright ©1986, United States Catholic Conference (USCC). Used with permission.

Soar we now: Music can be found in *The Hymnal 1982* #188 and #189.

DAY 40

I will give: Revelation 2:10.

Queen of heaven: The Regina Caeli from *A Book of Prayers.* Copyright ©1982, International Committee on English in the Liturgy, Inc. (ICEL). All rights reserved.

We sing of God: Music can be found in *The Hymnal 1982* #386 and #387.

Another distinctive: From *The Sacramental Mysteries*, edited by Casimir Kucharek, 1976. Used by permission of the publisher, Alleluia Press, Allendale NJ.

Day 41

A shield: Psalm 7:11.

I renounce thee: From *Documents of the Baptismal Liturgy* by E. G. Whitaker. Used by permission of S.P.C.K., London.

Let us: From *Baptism*, edited by Andre Hamman. Published by Alba House, a division of the Society of St. Paul, Staten Island NY. Used with permission.

Quickly the knight: From *St. George and the Dragon*, retold by Margaret Hodges. Text copyright ©1984, Margaret Hodges.

Done is the battle: From *The New Oxford Book of Christian Verse*, edited by Donald Davie. Oxford University Press, 1981.

Guide me ever: Music can be found in *Lutheran Book of Worship* #343.

Day 42

The angel: Revelation 22:1.

Awe-inspiring: From *The Mass*, edited by Adalbert Hamman. Published by Alba House, a division of the Society of St. Paul, Staten Island NY. Used with permission.

How well I know: From *The Poems of St. John of the Cross*, edited by Willis Barnstone. Copyright ©1968, Indiana University Press. Used by permission of New Direction Publishing Corp.

Bearing life: From *Pascha: The Resurrection of Christ*. Published by St. Vladimir's Seminary Press, Crestwood NY, 1980. Used with permission.

I've just: Music can be found in *Lead Me, Guide Me* #110.

Then John saw: From *Go Tell It on the Mountain* by James Baldwin. Copyright 1952, 1953, James Baldwin. Reprinted by permission of Doubleday, a division of Bantam, Doubleday, Dell Publishing Group, Inc.

For it is: From *The Liturgy of the Hours*. Copyright ©1974, International Committee on English in the Liturgy, Inc. (ICEL). All rights reserved.

Seventh Week of Easter

Day 43

We are: 2 Corinthians 6:16.

May is: From *The Poems of Gerard Manley Hopkins*, fourth edition, edited by W. H. Gardner and N. H. Mackenzie. Published by Oxford University Press, New York, 1967.

Day 44

May we: Psalm 65:5.

When everyone: From *Springtime of the Liturgy* by Lucien Deiss, translated by Matthew J. O'Connell. Copyright ©1979, The Order of St. Benedict, Inc. Published by The Liturgical Press, Collegeville MN. Used with permission.

The higher: From *Holy the Firm* by Annie Dillard. Published by Harper and Row Publishers.

Christians are: From *The Liturgy of the Hours*. Copyright ©1974, International Committee on English in the Liturgy, Inc. (ICEL). All rights reserved.

Day 45

I saw water: Ezekiel 47:1.

Whenever water: From *Visions of Seminars* by C. G. Jung, vol. 2, notes of Mary Foote. Published by Spring Publications, Zurich, 1976.

But the Christian: From *For the Life of the World: Sacraments and Orthodoxy* by Alexander Schmemann. St. Vladimir's Seminary Press, Crestwood NJ, 1973. Used with permission.

More was involved: From *The Shape of Baptism* by Aidan Kavanagh, OSB. Copyright ©1978, Pueblo Publishing Company, Inc. Used with permission.

Day 46

Then will I: Psalm 43:4.

Look with favor: From the English translation of Eucharistic Prayer I (Roman Canon) from *The Roman Missal*. Copyright ©1973, International Committee on English in the Liturgy, Inc. (ICEL). All rights reserved.

DAY 47

You yourselves: Isaiah 61:6.

Jesus Christ: From *Springtime of the Liturgy* by Lucien Deiss, translated by Matthew J. O'Connell. Copyright ©1979, The Order of St. Benedict, Inc. Published by The Liturgical Press, Collegeville MN. Used with permission.

Come, Almighty: Music can be found in *Lutheran Book of Worship* #315.

As kingfishers: From *The Poems of Gerard Manley Hopkins*, fourth edition, edited by W. H. Gardner and N. H. MacKenzie. Published by Oxford University Press, New York, 1967.

On praying: From *Signs, Words, and Gestures* by Balthasar Fischer. Copyright ©1981, Pueblo Publishing Company, Inc. Used with permission.

What we: From *The Liturgy of the Hours*. Copyright ©1974, International Committee on English in the Liturgy, Inc. (ICEL). All rights reserved.

DAY 48

In the daytime: Exodus 40:38.

Now you say: From *The Cloud of Unknowing*, edited by William Johnston. Copyright ©1973, William Johnston. Used by permission of Doubleday, a division of Bantam, Doubleday, Dell Publishing Group.

Whenever a real: From *Signs, Words, and Gestures* by Balthasar Fischer. Copyright ©1981, Pueblo Publishing Company, Inc. Used with permission.

DAY 49

All you: Daniel 3:65,66.

Every time: Music can be found in *Lead Me, Guide Me* #220.

You are a fire: From *Catherine of Siena, The Dialogue* translated by Suzanne Noffke. From the Classics of Western Spirituality Series. Copyright ©1980, Missionary Society of St. Paul the Apostle in the State of New York. Used by permission of Paulist Press.

He who saved: From *Pascha: The Resurrection of Christ*. Published by St. Vladimir's Seminary Press, Crestwood NY, 1980. Used with permission.

None other Lamb: From *A Treasury of Poems for Worship and Devotion*, edited by Charles L. Wallis. Harper and Row Publishers.

O ardent fire: From *Medieval Women's Visionary Literature*, edited by Elizabeth Alvilda Petroff. Copyright ©1986, Oxford University Press. Used with permission.

Come, Holy Spirit: From *A Book of Prayers*. Copyright ©1982, International Committee on English in the Liturgy, Inc. (ICEL). All rights reserved.

Holy breathing: From *It's Midnight, Lord* by Dom Helder Camara, translated by Joseph Gallagher with Thomas Fuller and Tom Conry. Copyright ©1984. Used by permission of The Pastoral Press, Washington DC. All rights reserved.

Pentecost

DAY 50

I saw: Revelation 21:2.

Wake, O wake: By Philipp Nicolai, translated and adapted by Christopher Idle. Copyright ©1982, Hope Publishing Company, Carol Stream IL. All rights reserved. Used with permission.

The death of Jesus: From *Economic Justice for All: Catholic Social Teaching and the U.S. Economy*. Copyright ©1986, United States Catholic Conference (USCC). Used with permission.

Holy Spirit: Translation by Peter Scagnelli.

For fifty days: From *For the Life of the World: Sacraments and Orthodoxy* by Alexander Schmemann. St. Vladimir's Seminary Press, Crestwood NY, 1973.

You, O Christ: From *Hymns of Divine Love, St. Symeon the New Theologian*, translated by George A. Maloney, SJ. Copyright ©1977, Dimension Books, Denville NJ. Used with permission.

Hope, Life, Way: From *Springtime of the Liturgy*, by Lucien Deiss, translated by Matthew J. O'Connell. Copyright ©1979, The Order of St. Benedict, Inc. Published by The Liturgical Press, Collegeville MN. Used with permission.

An Order for Daily Prayer

The psalms from *The Psalms: A New Translation for Prayer and Worship* by Gary Chamberlain. Copyright ©1984, The Upper Room. Used by permission of the author. All rights reserved.

Canticle translations and prayer texts by Gail Ramshaw and Gordon Lathrop.